ALL ABOUT CHILDREN

All About Children

John Inchley

COVERDALE HOUSE PUBLISHERS
LONDON AND EASTBOURNE

ISBN 0 902088 92 0

Printed in Great Britain for Coverdale House Publishers Ltd., Lottbridge Drove, Eastbourne, East Sussex BN23 6NT by Hunt Barnard Printing Ltd., Aylesbury, Bucks.

To my wife Mary, my step-sons Michael and Brian, and my daughters Carol and Rosemary, who have all contributed in so many different ways to the making of this book.

Contents

Introduction

'Your children are not your children.
They are the sons and daughters of Life's longing for itself.
They come through you but not from you,
And though they are with you yet they belong not to you.
You may give them your love but not your thoughts,
For they have their own thoughts.
You may house their bodies but not their souls,
For their souls dwell in the house of tomorrow, which you
    cannot visit, not even in your dreams.
You may strive to be like them, but seek not to make them
    like you.
For life goes not backward nor tarries with yesterday.
You are the bows from which your children as living arrows
    are sent forth.
The Archer sees the mark on the path of the infinite,
And he bends you with his might that his arrows may go
    swift and far.
Let your bending in the Archer's hand be for gladness;
For even as he loves the arrow that flies,
So he loves the bow that is stable.'[1]

This book is all about children.

It is written with a desire to help parents and teachers, as
well as ministers, to fulfil their God-given responsibility of
bringing up boys and girls in the discipline and instruction of
the Lord.

It is about all children, including infants, but particularly
boys and girls of seven to eleven. And it will examine what

the Bible teaches about the spiritual relationship of such children to God and their response to God and His call.

The book is written with the conviction that 'while children have to be told that they must wait before they can fulfil life's great responsibilities, Jesus needs them now and they need him, and they can be as real and true Christians as grown up people.'

Here is a quote from a report on evangelism called 'Towards the Conversion of England': 'In the case of a definite call to decide for Christ, undue pressure and unwise emotion should be scrupulously avoided; but it should come to every child before the change from primary to secondary education.'[2]

During recent years, many seriously-minded Christians have been fiighting shy of even the most orthodox forms of children's evangelism. They are instinctively unhappy about the conviction widely held, that children are born into the world in a state of being not only guilty, but lost, and that it is a first responsibility of parents and teachers to lead them to salvation.

Worldwide committees are meeting, and regular conferences are being held in order to produce an agreed scriptural working basis which can be truly acceptable. As this is happening, many Christian parents are becoming increasingly uneasy and concerned about their traditional beliefs and the teaching of the Church with regard to the relationship of their children to the Lord.

There has always been concern on the part of thinking people about children who die. What do we, as Christian workers, say to them? Can we speak helpfully and with authority to both Christian and non-Christian parents alike regarding the state of the children who have been taken from them by accident or sickness? Then there is the problem of the mentally handicapped. What are we to believe about these? Many thinking people are unsure in their minds as to whether children from Christian families have special advantages over boys and girls whose parents remain unbelievers. 'And,' some regularly ask, 'why do so many children of believing parents appear to reject the faith of their fathers?'

In order to find the answers we must be willing to turn our backs on traditional belief. To hold tenaciously to the things that have been handed down to us, does not mean that we are necessarily right. It is useful to remember that much closely guarded traditional thinking does not go back nearly as far as we often imagine.

We must also be willing to break away from denominational intolerance and prejudice even though our subject cannot entirely be divorced from the practices of infant, family or believer's baptism. I have no desire to argue for one or the other. Each must decide about this for himself. It is important that our loyalty to one or the other practice does not sidetrack us from the main issue.

I shall quote from different sources and the reader must be careful not to reject theological evidence simply because the presenter has beliefs different from his own. I have no cause to champion. Rest assured my aim is to guard the happiness of the children and to encourage their freedom from the tensions that could so easily come from the constant badgering of a well meaning but misguided adult world.

There is a need in our day and generation for ministers and teachers to hear afresh the call from our Lord himself to let the children come to him for to such belongs the Kingdom of Heaven. We must be stirred by the provocative charge of Psalm 78 concerning the great Bible truths which we have heard and known: 'We will not hide them from their children, we will tell to the coming generation the glorious deeds of the Lord, and his might, and the wonders which he has wrought ... so that they should set their hope in God, and not forget the works of God, but keep his commandments.'

The prayer of my heart is that God will be pleased to use this book to stir the hearts of Christian people to give them a new vision of the importance of children to our Heavenly Father.

Chapter One

CHILD STATUS

It is sad to hear Christian parents declaring– 'John is saved, though Mary isn't, and we are not quite sure about Bill.' They speak of their own children, all under the age of twelve, who are completely aware of what is being said, and they react accordingly.

What a difference it would make if they were treated as belonging to the Lord from the very beginning. Parents should exercise faith in the promises of God and in the atoning work of Christ on behalf of their sons and daughters, believing in the unity of the family. God himself has ordained this to be the organic channel of spiritual life to every member, both young and old alike.

In this chapter I hope to indicate what is the developmental status of all children during the years of infancy and childhood and before the age of accountability. Experience shows that this is an area in which very many Christian parents and teachers are seeking assurance.

We begin with the following fundamental questions.

1. Do I believe that no children, or only some, really belong to God until they have said 'Yes' to Jesus Christ, or can I happily believe that all children belong to God until such time as they may say 'No?'

2. Must I act towards boys and girls as if they are essentially lost, and be anxiously working to get them into the Kingdom or may I be assured that all children belong to the Kingdom of God, be positive and relaxed in teaching them objectively about the Lord and his ways so that they may accept *them* in God's own time?

3. Must I be constantly striving, praying and hoping that they may qualify to have their names written in God's Book of Life or may I dare to believe that their names are already there, and be praying and believing that from their earliest days they will make a happy, positive response to the Lord Himself, that their names may never be blotted out?[1]

Whatever subject we may be studying, it is important to be absolutely correct in the fundamental premise. It is just here that many orthodox Christians go astray in their approach towards the spiritual needs of boys and girls, and in their beliefs regarding their spiritual status.

The basic mistake is to suppose that what is true of adults is also true of children. I am grateful for a statement by a modern theologian who declares, 'Evangelicalism's criminal attitude to children can only be understood when the extent to which it is imprisoned in an adult-orientated theology is grasped.'[2]

This mistaken adult approach to children will be dealt with more fully in subsequent chapters, but there are three fundamental errors which should be recognized immediately.

1. There is the mistaken application to children of the guilt which belongs exclusively to wilful heart's rebellion towards God. A child is incapable of this before the age of responsibility. This is no denial of the existence of original sin as we shall see later.

2. There follows the application to the child of a consequential state of being lost from God. As far as children are concerned this is completely untrue.

3. The final result of this damaging adult-theology approach is the constant appeal to children to be saved through repentance and faith. There is usually an insistence on a real conviction of sin and all too often an emphasis on a once for all commitment.

We must not cling to such adult orientated theology for if we do the very basis of our beliefs regarding the children will be unscriptural. We must discover a new way to assess the spiritual status of the child.

It needs to be realized that misguided adults can so often bring unhappiness to a child. A proper approach can do just the opposite. Let me give examples of this.

The first concerns a woman who once said to me, 'when I was a child I was constantly asked if I had given my heart to Jesus. If I had said, 'No', it would have involved me in further embarrassment so I usually said, 'Yes'. After this I was questioned as to when I had taken the step and I would reply that it had happened in Sunday school. I was then asked if I had told my teacher and I would answer that I hadn't. It was suggested that I should tell her as it would make her very happy.'

'The fact was,' said my friend, 'I had always loved Jesus for as long as I could remember, just as I had always loved my parents.'

This worrying of a child about her response to the Lord is most regrettable, as is the suggestion that she would make some adult happy by telling of the happening.

For a contrasting and invigorating alternative we should consider the following dedication written by Dr Campbell Morgan for his book, 'The Crises of the Christ.'[3]

'TO MY FATHER AND MOTHER,
Who forty years ago gave me to Christ, and who never doubting
the acceptance by HIM of their child,
did from infancy, and through youth, train me as HIS,
from whom I received my first knowledge of HIM,
so that when the necessity came for my personal choosing,
so did I recognize the claims of HIS love, that without
revulsion, and hardly knowing when,
I YIELDED TO HIM
my allegiance and my love, devoting spirit, soul, and body
to HIS sweet will and glad service;
in thankfulness to them for their earliest teaching,

and continuance of revelation of HIM by example,
in many differing circumstances,
in which their loyalty to HIM
was a perpetual witness to my heart,
of the perfection of HIS love;
in thankfulness that they are still with me
labouring together in prayer,
I DEDICATE THIS BOOK.'

In order to safeguard myself from misunderstanding and to be disassociated from the error of baptismal regeneration, let me say at the outset that basically we must think of the actual spiritual status of the child quite apart from baptism, though the importance and significance of baptism for the sealing of the status will be given its proper place later in the chapter.

The importance of the alternative approach may be set out as follows.

1. First of all, it required us to believe that Jesus meant what he said when He declared that the Kingdom of Heaven belongs to *all children*.

2. Secondly it required us to believe that *all children*, before the age of responsibility, even bearing in mind their link with Adam's sin, are covered objectively by the atoning work of Christ. They belong to God until such time as they may deliberately refuse him. This means that during their growing-up years, they are completely outside the judgement of God.

3. Thirdly it requires us to agree that there is a special sense of belonging for the children of godly parents, and even for those who come from non-Christian or nominally Christian homes if they enjoy the spiritual care and instruction that comes from godly Sunday school teachers and Bible class leaders.

4. Without denominational bias we are to believe that the children of Christian parents, and many of those from non-Christian homes who are properly taught, are likely to be unconsciously regenerated by the sovereign activity of the Holy Spirit during infancy or early childhood. The adult

graces of repentance and faith may not yet have been formed in them, but the seeds of both, and indeed of other needful graces, will have been planted in their hearts by the same secret operation of the Holy Spirit.

5. We are permitted, therefore, to expect that there will be a developing consciousness for the growing child, either declared or undeclared, of love and trust towards God, and a real sense of belonging. This can be enjoyed together by all the members of a Christian family, and there will be no rejection of any, simply because they have not as yet made a stereotyped acknowledgment of any conscious belief.

It is possible that some readers may not previously have met this so-called new approach, which is in fact authenticated by both the Old and New Testaments and has been propounded by Bible expositors from the earliest times. If this should be so, I pray that it may not be lightly rejected, or thought to be absurd. It must not be thought that the Spirit of God is unable to work in such a manner for the provision of his salvation for infants and children.

When writing about the reasonableness of the regeneration of infants (not baptismal regeneration) Calvin said 'The work of God is not yet without existence because it is not observed or understood by us.'[4]

Throughout the whole of this study we shall need to bear in mind that there will be differences of approach in the consideration of the children who are fortunate enough to benefit from belonging to Christian families or the care and teaching of godly teachers and those who are not. In the list, already given, we have included declarations which belong to *all children,* yet it is evident that there is this special sense of belonging for boys and girls who are fortunate enough to possess a Christian background. We shall return to the wider situation towards the end of the chapter.

In order to appreciate more fully this childhood orientated approach to the spiritual status of boys and girls, especially of those who benefit from a godly background, we may consider the physical and spiritual development of some of the children of the Bible. Let us begin with the child Samuel. We must appreciate that this boy's conscious dramatic call by Jehovah, and his subsequent response, were all part of his growing up as a child who had been given in faith to the Lord by his godly mother (See 1 Sam 1:26–28).

Notice carefully the Bible sequence 'And the boy Samuel grew in the presence of the Lord.' (1 Sam 2:21)

'Now the boy Samuel continued to grow both in stature and in favour with the Lord and with men.' (1 Sam. 2:26)

'Now Samuel did not yet know the Lord, and the word of the Lord had not been revealed to him.' (1 Sam. 3:7)

It is important to appreciate that while he 'did not yet know the Lord' that is, intelligently for himself, he was already 'in favour with the Lord.' 'And Samuel said, "Speak for your servant hears." ' (1 Sam. 3:10)

'And Samuel grew and the Lord was with him and let none of his words fall to the ground.' (1 Sam. 3:19)

Here is a scriptural pattern for every Christian child growing up happily in a Godly environment and liberated from constant appeals to 'Come to Jesus.' Set free from the necessity of such adult promptings, he is likely to make a succession of responses, as no doubt the child Samuel did, which can be epitomized by the classic, 'Speak for your servant hears.'

The study of Samuel's experience also provides us with an awareness that just as the normal child's state of physical and mental progression is perfectly suited to his present chronological age and environmental needs and relationships, so his spiritual progression is essential to his developing relationship with God. Physically, intellectually and spiritually, we have a series of 'unfoldings', never exactly the same for each child, and always adapted to the need of the present.

Just as a normal child of any age is physically and intellectually complete, so the same child can be spiritually whole at any age. And let us always remember that there is an infinite variety in maturity. Just as there is no exact age when a child walks or talks, so there is no exact age when he begins to pray or read the Bible on his own, or when he is likely to say Yes or No consciously to God.

Look once again at the recorded statements about the physical and spiritual progress of Samuel.

'And the boy Samuel grew in the presence of the Lord.'

'Now the boy Samuel continued to grow both in stature and in favour with the Lord and with men.'

'And Samuel grew and the Lord was with him.'

Now compare Campbell Morgan's testimony of his growing-up experience in a relaxed Godly home, 'My mother and father gave me to Christ. They never doubted the acceptance by him of their child. From infancy and through youth they trained me as his. With the result that when the necessity came for my personal choosing, so did I recognize the claims of His love, that without revulsion and hardly knowing when, I yielded to Him my allegiance and my love.'

Side by side with these two accounts it is interesting and important to compare Luke 1:80 which tells of the physical and spiritual development of the boy who became John the Baptist.

'And the child grew and became strong in spirit.'

Becoming strong in spirit was co-existent with his growing strong in body as, indeed, it was with the child Samuel, and with young Campbell Morgan.

Later on Luke writes similarly and sensitively of the physical growth of the boy Jesus.

'And the child grew and became strong, filled with wisdom; and the favour of God was upon Him.'

'And Jesus increased in wisdom and stature, and in favour with God and men.' (Luke 2:40 & 52).

Even for the sinless Son of God it is recorded that there was an increase in wisdom and favour with God which occurred at the same time as his physical growth. It is only in the apocryphal writings that we find him irreverently turned into an infant prodigy.

So we find Calvin writing that 'Christ was sanctified from

His earliest infancy that He might sanctify all His elect.'[5] And we may profitably recall these well known words of Mrs Alexander written a hundred years ago:-

'For He is our childhood's pattern,
Day by day like us He grew.'

A careful comparison of all these case histories should enable us to appreciate the importance of this Biblical concept of a developing spiritual experience for children. We must therefore avoid evangelicalism's criminal attitude towards them when it says this or that one is not a Christian, because he has not outwardly conformed to some adult pattern of declared and conscious repentance and faith.

With children of Christian families in mind a writer of a hundred years ago put it like this, 'While you may declare concerning inanimate things that this is gold and that is stone and this is lead and so on, are you equally able to say with confidence that at any moment of physical growth that this is a lamb and that is a sheep, or this is a colt and that is a horse, or even that this is a child and that is a man? A colt is potentially a horse and a child is potentially an adult. This is the law of futuration.

'The spiritual futuration of a Christian child does not lie in what an infant does or does not consciously believe, or can or cannot believe, but in the covenant of promise which makes his parents parents in the Lord; and his nurture a nurture of the Lord; constituting a force of futuration by which he is to grow up imperceptibly into the Lord as a faithful among faithfuls.'[6]

This brings us to the all important subject of covenant relationship. Whilst we shall deal more fully with this in another chapter, it is important at this stage to have its reality and significance in mind. We must appreciate how close is the link that exists between all parents whether Christian or non-Christian and their children. The nature and character of a family are God-given qualities that are essential for the proper development of the personalities of each of its members. The children cannot help but participate in the behaviour patterns of the home and it will be noticed how the Scriptures continually associate children with the character and destiny of their parents. So, ideally, the child's growing awareness of God is bound up in the living, pulsating relationships which should belong to every Christian home. Notice again the statement of the woman already mentioned, regarding her childhood experience, 'I had always loved Jesus for as long as I could remember just as I had always loved my parents.' So, God is the child's Heavenly Father and to honour parents is in fact to honour God.

Marcel writes, 'In God's eyes parents and their children are *one*. By divine right the parents are the authorized representatives of their children; they act for them; they engage in spiritual responsibilities because of them and for them and also in their name. Such is the order of God.'[7]

Bushnell is even more forthright, 'Understand that it is the family spirit, the organic life of the house, the silent power of a domestic godliness, working, as it does, unconsciously and with sovereign effect – this is it which forms your children to God. And, if this be wanting, all that you may do beside, will be as likely to annoy and harden as to bless.'[8]

For children growing up with any kind of Christian background there should, ideally, be no crisis experience, only a maturing appreciation of what has been happening. Sometimes this awareness comes quite suddenly and dramatically and so it appears to be an experience of conversion, and there is surely no harm in calling it this. It is much better, however, if the eventual grown-up conscious and intelligent commitment to Christ is the culmination of a warm and growing relationship with God not unlike the child's growing love and appreciation of its natural parents. As a girl of eleven or twelve wrote recently to me during one of my missions, 'I have believed in Jesus for as long as I can remember, only I said a very special "Yes", on Monday'.

It is because of a rigid adherence to the traditional beliefs that so many of us have failed to appreciate that there is an age of intelligent responsibility for conscious acceptance or rejection of truth by the individual. This is why so many of the doctrines that belong to older people who have definitely and consciously rejected Christ are applied to boys and girls who as yet have not rejected Him. As far as we know they may not have said 'Yes' to Jesus consciously, but they have certainly not said 'No'.

Turn now to the statements about belief and unbelief found in John 3:16–21. It is basic to our understanding of this key passage of New Testament doctrine that we appreciate that both believing and unbelieving are definite and critical happenings in time. The light will need to have been revealed in some form or other in order for there to be an obligation on the part of the individual to accept it or reject it.

This clearly means that anyone, and particularly a child, is not necessarily an unbeliever because he has not yet consciously believed. It is likely that he may be a non-believer or a not-yet-believer which is quite different.[9] He may even be an embryonic or immature believer; someone who has loved Jesus for as long as he can remember. He has quite happily responded to the light which he has received, but with an incomplete appreciation of the meaning of things such as repentance and faith.

On the other hand, an unbeliever who is 'condemned already' is one who has wilfully set himself in the way of darkness rather than light because his deeds are evil. He has definitely said 'No' to God by his attitude and behaviour which are quite removed from a child's unsophisticated naughtiness and unintended wrongdoing. It is wilful heart rebellion towards God and his Christ which exposes the individual to the judgment of Jehovah. Compare Christ's own words recorded in John 16:9 and 15:22 ' ... of sin because they do not believe in me'. And, 'If I had not come and spoken to them, they would not have sin: but now they have no excuse for their sin'. The light must come in some form or other before judgment is declared against those who love the darkness rather than the light.

Sooner or later, of course, a refusal to say a definite Yes by those who have received the light will be tantamount to saying No. We must teach this to all, especially to the older children. At the same time we must be careful not to condemn any child simply because he has not yet made this kind of conscious response.

One of the great evangelistic challenges of our time is that there *are* children as well as adults, who would seem by their behaviour patterns to be deliberately rejecting God, and setting themselves in the ways of darkness rather than light. It may be that these too must be classed as unbelievers, though we must be extremely careful in our analysis and judgment even of these, and be prayerfully exercised for their salvation.

We have already noticed that there cannot possibly be anything static about anyone's response to God and to Jesus Christ. Believing for both young and old, in the true Biblical sense, must always possess the qualities of growth and vitality. For some it will certainly begin with a crisis, but if it is real, the crisis will immediately become a developing process. It will be a *living* faith.

For children brought up within a Christian home the reality of intelligent response with or without a crisis experience, is likely to occur at any time between the ages of six and eleven, or maybe even earlier. It will be a culmination of much that has gone before, whether unconsciously or subconsciously in the mind of the child. The question to ask such children, and adults for that matter, is not, 'Have you believed?' but rather, 'Do you believe?' or 'Are you believing?'

I once asked a boy of thirteen who was enquiring about

church membership if he had said Yes to Jesus Christ. He said he had not. 'Well then, have you said no,' I asked. 'Certainly not,' he replied, 'and what is more I don't mean to.' In a few days time, having been shown the way more clearly he voluntarily told me that he had made a conscious and positive response to the Saviour.

I believe that this boy had unconsciously said yes long before this, as so many children do. Then came a moment during a time of mission, when he was able personally to enter into the conscious experience of positive belonging. Now he is witnessing in the church, and quietly (or perhaps still a bit noisily!) growing up in the ways of the Lord. The important thing to notice about such noisy, irresponsible, lovable boys, is that their attitude is not usually one of rejection or rebellion towards the Lord.

I want now to call two witnesses from the past to support what I feel is so important. One is an Anglican and the other a well known, highly esteemed member of the Christian Brethren.

Dr Griffith Thomas is the Anglican. Forty years or so ago he was Rector of St. Paul's Church, Portman Square in London and later, Principal of Wycliffe Hall, Oxford, and was a great Bible scholar. I quote from his book, *The Principles of Theology* published in 1930 and written as an introduction to the Thirty Nine Articles of the Church of England. Concerning Article IX of Original Birth Sin Dr Thomas says, 'Children are born with an evil nature in a state of what is called depravity, and when reason dawns they know something of right and wrong, though they have only a partial responsibility, but in course of time they become fully responsible for the sin of their own will.'[10]

He goes on to point out that 'original sin' is not a biblical phrase, and that he prefers 'inborn sinfulness' to describe the principle of evil which, by reason of the connection of the race with Adam, has infected human nature. He then continues,

'Adam's posterity stands just where he stood after the Fall. And now Christ the last Adam meets and more than meets the sin and guilt of the first Adam (Romans 5:12 & 19; 1 Cor. 15:22).'[11] He goes on to discuss God's wrath and damnation towards original sin, and then quotes from Litton, 'In whomsoever, therefore it is found, even as a latent potentiality, it must *in itself* be an object of God's displeasure; but it does not mean that the person must be so ... so that the infant himself if he dies as an infant, is not, and never has been an object of God's wrath'.[12]

Dr Thomas returns to this important subject in his dealing with Article XXVI, and speaks about 'the exact relation of unconscious childhood to the Atonement of Christ'.

'Whether we think of children dying or living,' he says, 'the fact is the same. What is the spiritual position of these infants in relation to our Lord? *Surely the truth is that all children are included in the great atoning sacrifice, and belong to Jesus Christ until they deliberately refuse Him.*'[13] This final sentence beautifully crystallizes what I am trying to say.

We now turn to the evidence happily provided by the beloved Christian Brother, George Goodman. This profound biblical teacher, a contemporary of Griffith Thomas, was one of the founders of Caravan Mission To Village Children and an active honorary worker and leader in the Children's Special Service Mission. He wrote numerous books, many of them in connection with children's evangelism. One was called, 'The Present State and Future Destiny of the Heathen'[14] in which he deals with the question of the condemnation of God towards all human beings, including children, who have a measure of irresponsibility. He arrives at the same conclusion as that categorically reached by Griffith Thomas. He sums up his argument as follows, 'In resurrection all stand upon their own responsibility to be dealt with, not for the sin of their Federal Head (i.e. Adam) but according for their own works as many passages tell us will be the case (Rom. 2:6; 2 Thess. 1:8). There is of course no question of any second chance in this. It is this life that determines all. The question is, on what ground does the judgment proceed? Surely the result must be:

1. That all irresponsible persons (infants and others) will have no charge against them and can therefore be the objects of that free grace that comes through the reconciliation made at Calvary. The gifts of salvation and eternal life may justly be extended to them, since where there is no law there is no transgression. (Rom. 4:15 and 5:13)

2. That the Second Death, that is the casting of both body and soul into Hell, of which Jesus spoke in such solemn terms, of which we read in Revelation 20:15: 'Whosoever was not found written in the book of life was cast into the Lake of Fire', is not for Adam's transgressions, but because of the personal sin of rejection of the proffered salvation in Christ. The Christ rejecter is the one upon whom the Second Death has power. 'This is the condemnation, that light is come into the world, and men loved darkness rather than light because their deeds were evil' (Jn. 3:19). It is these lovers of the dark who are cast into outer darkness.

So we find these acknowledged biblical teachers both expressing the same belief. Griffith Thomas says, '*All* children are included in the great atoning sacrifice, and belong to Jesus Christ until they deliberately refuse Him.'

Whilst George Goodman writes, '*Infants* can be the objects of that free grace that comes through the reconciliation made at Calvary . . . the Christ rejector is the one upon whom the Second Death has power.'

If we dare to believe these two great evangelical-biblical teachers, then we must re-think our whole spiritual approach to boys and girls both in our families and in the church. The new proposition will be:

We believe that all children are included in the great atoning sacrifice and belong to Jesus Christ until they deliberately refuse Him.

This will immediately mean that for the boys and girls there will be a new happy experience of belonging. We shall also be able to speak confidently and comfortingly to parents and friends concerning children who have died as well as those who are living, and concerning individuals who are mentally handicapped, or for some other reason are irresponsible.

There is likely to be a radical change in our general approach to the children for whom we have special responsibilities, and a mutual deepening of our personal relationship and sympathetic understanding. Instead of ostracizing them as individuals who are lost and perishing, we will think of them as those who belong. We shall constantly remember that they are the special objects of God's loving concern and care during their growing up years. Instead of worrying them all the time to be saved, we must be telling them more and more about God and His Son. We shall be telling of Christ's character, His love and His work.

Our teaching concerning the cross and resurrection, and the work of the Holy Spirit will be much more objective. We must speak with stronger emphasis of the availability of forgiveness rather than the final judgment of sin. When speaking to children we must emphasize the second half of Romans 6:23 that the gift of God is eternal life rather than that the wages of sin is death.

We must not neglect to teach the importance of conscious response, though this will be in the context of appropriating something which has already been given, the personal possession and enjoyment of an inheritance to which the child already has a title. We must always remember that this response is likely to be a developmental experience compatible and co-existent with the physical and mental development of the growing child.

During the years that precede a declaration of conscious and personal response we must avoid any form of worrying or pressure, or any attitude of spiritual apartheid towards the children. Most of all we must resist the temptation of saying that this one is converted or saved and that one is not.

We shall also find ourselves telling the children much more of what the Lord Jesus can be to them, and do for them here and now, rather than continually teaching about the hereafter and harping on the importance of 'getting a ticket to heaven'.

The loving relationship that exists between God and the child may be rejected by the growing boy or girl, but if we are patient and prayerful in our teaching we may expect to see a happy and growing response which will be consummated, in God's own time in the experience of regeneration and in an eternal relationship – belonging to God forever.

It is because of this acknowledgment of belonging, that believing parents make sure that their sons and daughters are dedicated or baptized in infancy. It is interesting to notice that there are parents belonging to the Christian Brethren who practise Infant baptism or Household baptism, whilst there are Anglican parents who prefer to dedicate their infants, leaving baptism for the child's later years when he can in his own right commit himself to God. Each one of us must be convinced in his own mind concerning one practice or the other.

For myself I have come to believe that in infant baptism there is a happy and scripturally important sealing of the blessings of belonging and of all the promises of God, even to the child of one believing parent. Though I recall that Archbishop William Temple was careful to say, 'We ought to recognize that the justification (i.e. for baptism administered in infancy) though abundant, is not evident'.[15] It is not my concern at this time to argue one way or the other.

All too often the contention between Christians on this matter has tended to sidetrack from the main issue. It will be more profitable if we can agree to differ amicably.

Let there be either baptism or dedication, and with it a sincere committing of the child's spiritual future to the love and care of God. I am, of course, aware that if all children belong (and I am insisting they do) then they should all be eligible for baptism or dedication. This, however, is a parent–child responsibility. When a child of non-Christian parents is adopted by believers, he is rightly either dedicated or baptized. We shall later deal more fully with the attitude to be adopted by responsible Christians towards the children who still belong to non-Christian families.

It is also sensible to receive children to the Lord's Supper. I appreciated the reality of this when visiting a large church in Toronto where children happily and reverently received the bread and wine together with their parents. As to what extent this practice will be generally accepted in our United Kingdom churches is the present concern of many who are able to judge better than I.

Finally it must be acknowledged that there are some orthodox Bible students who, whilst they are willing to allow what has been said to apply to the children of Christian parents, are reluctant to permit any part of it to include the greater number of children whose parents are not Christians. This includes the many millions of children in this country and overseas whose parents belong to a heathen religion. It would seem that we are faced with three alternatives:

1. To condemn all the children of non-Christian families to eternal torment should they die without positive faith in Christ.

2. To accept the teaching of conditional immortality and so believe that a child brought up without a Christian background has no further existence after final judgment. Many more have subscribed to this school of thought for responsible adults since the publication of *The Righteous Judge* by H. E. Guillebaud and *Life and Immortality* by Basil Atkinson.[17]

3. To be committed and to hide behind the faithful declaration of Jehovah to Abraham of old. (Genesis 18) 'Shall not the judge of all the earth do right?' This statement was made in a completely different context and to quote it here, is to say the least, unsatisfactory.

Let me say quite positively that I share the conclusion expressed by Griffith Thomas and George Goodman. I cannot help but believe that all children belong to the Lord before the age of accountability. Their inborn sinfulness is covered by the atoning work of Christ, and their acts of wrongdoing, which have not been committed wilfully, may also be covered by the Atonement even though this has not yet been appropriated by an act of will. I firmly believe that *All children are included in the great atoning sacrifice, and belong to Jesus Christ until they deliberately refuse Him.* I have arrived at this conclusion after many years of careful thought and prayerful study of the arguments put forward and of the scriptures quoted, remembering particularly what Jesus said in Matthew chapters 18 and 19 and again in Mark and Luke of the relationship of children to Himself.

Chapter Two

OF SUCH IS THE KINGDOM

In chapters 18 and 19 of Matthew's Gospel and the corresponding passages in Mark 10 and Luke 18, we have recorded the words and acts of Jesus himself which encourage us to believe that all children are both important and acceptable to our Heavenly Father. We are encouraged to believe that, given the opportunity, these boys and girls are likely to make an early response to the Good News of God. It is the words and acts of Jesus which provide us with his authority for an active and expectant ministry towards children both in the home and the church. It is important to study these chapters with a modern translation of the Bible for reference.

We begin with verses 13 to 15 of Matthew chapter 19 and quote in full. 'Then children were brought to him that he might lay his hands on them and pray. The disciples rebuked the people; but Jesus said, "Let the children come to me, and do not hinder them – for to such belongs the kingdom of heaven". And he laid his hands on them and went away.'

These children were probably very young. In Luke 18 they are called babes. William Barclay tells us that it was the custom of mothers to bring their boys and girls to some distinguished Rabbi on their first birthday that he might bless them. Jesus took them up in his arms and blessed them. (See Mark 10). This too suggests younger children. The word used in Matthew 19, however, is *paidion* in the Greek and is a word used when speaking of both older and younger children up to the age of twelve; the daughter of Jairus for example. In all three Gospels Jesus uses this word for those to whom the Kingdom of Heaven belongs. The New English Bible and the Revised Standard Version translate the word, *'children'* and not 'little children', as in the King James Version. It is not unreasonable, therefore, to suppose that although this historic statement was uttered by our Lord probably in the context of blessing very young children, there is no exclusion of those who are older.

It can be argued, of course, that Jesus did not say 'to *all* such'. This however would seem to be implied.

There is no limitation suggested by Christ's introductory words, 'Let the children come'. The declaration that the Kingdom belongs to the children cannot be limited to those who come, or even to those who are brought. The straightforward meaning of the text is that we are to let *all* the children come *because* the Kingdom belongs to each of them.[1] To believe and teach that the Kingdom is only for those who come, is a misinterpretation of our Lord's direct teaching.

As we examine these affirmations of Jesus we must appreciate that the words that he *said* were spoken in the context of the things that He *did*, namely welcoming the children, encircling them with His arms and blessing them.

With these child-directed actions in mind let us now examine the added statement of Jesus on this occasion as recorded by Mark and Luke. 'Truly I say to you, whoever does not receive the kingdom of God like a child shall not enter it.' (Mk 10:15; Lk 18:17).

This statement is the reason given by some Christians for insisting that the previous declaration of Jesus, concerning the belonging of the Kingdom to children, is illustrative only, and not directly applicable to the boys and girls themselves, save in a very narrow sense.

They argue that these two words, 'of such' (K.J.V.) must be understood in the context of what Jesus said afterwards, and must refer only to older people who are prepared to become *like* children, and not to the children themselves. First of all, it should be clear in our minds that the absence of the second saying of Jesus from Matthew's gospel allows both sayings to be independent of each other. One cannot reasonably argue that in view of the second statement, the first statement does not apply directly to children, for this is entirely separate.

Jesus simply took advantage of the opportunity provided by this happening in the course of a day's ministry to illustrate a secondary truth. We find Him doing exactly the same kind of thing only in reverse in Matthew 18, where he begins by using the child as a visual aid for adult teaching and then, taking advantage of the occasion, he makes a number of important declarations concerning the children themselves. On this occasion when the children were brought by their mothers to him, and clearly responded to his welcome, he could not help remarking to the adults who were present, 'Look, this is the only way to enter into the kingdom *trustfully* just as these children are responding, physically, to my welcoming outstretched arms'.

But what He had said previously about the children themselves was something entirely different.

The words in the King James Version 'of such' can be rendered just as accurately 'to such' which is favoured by many of the more recent translators. The Revised Standard Version renders the verse in Matthew 19, 'to such belongs the kingdom of heaven', and the New English Bible, 'the Kingdom of Heaven belongs to such as these'. What, therefore, does 'to such' really mean? The Greek pronoun is the single word, *toioutos*. Its usage in the New Testament is literal, and not illustrative. Examples are as follows:

1. John 4:23, '... the true worshippers will worship the Father in spirit and in truth, for *such* the Father seeks to worship Him.'

2. Acts 22:22 'Away with *such* (a fellow) from the earth'. Notice that this refers to Paul himself as well as to others actually like him.

3. Gal. 6:1 'Brethren, if a man is overtaken in any trespass,

3

you who are spiritual should restore *him* in a spirit of gentleness'. Both the Authorized and Revized versions translate here, 'ye that are spiritual restore such an one . . .'[2] The meaning is clear. The pronoun is used thirteen times in the New Testament, and in every case it has a literal application.[3]

We may conclude, therefore, that on this important occasion when the children were brought to Jesus, and he identified Himself with them by putting His arms around them, that he meant exactly what he said. 'Let the children come to me; and do not hinder them; for to such (or, literally "to them" – see Gal. 6:1 above) belongs the Kingdom of Heaven.'

There is no suggestion here or anywhere else in the Scriptures that the Kingdom belongs either to children or to adults *because* they are trustful, or innocent, or humble, or receptive of loving.[4] It belongs to them entirely through the Grace of God, and because of the atoning work of Christ.

Intelligent adults cannot possibly be 'of such' unconditionally, because they *are* accountable.

It is important to notice that there is no doctrinal clash between the statement in the Synoptic Gospels of the Kingdom of God *belonging* to children, and our Lord's declaration to Nicodemus, recorded in John chapter 3, that the experience of *entering* the Kingdom is completely dependent upon the New Birth from above. Belonging and entering are two entirely different concepts.

It must always be remembered that, while it is convenient to think of the Kingdom of God or the Kingdom of Heaven (they are one) as being synonymous with the Church through which it is revealed and proclaimed, the Kingdom has a much wider meaning and field of operation.

It is not a territorial kingdom in any sense. Moffat in his translation of the Bible legitimately renders 'the Kingdom of God' as 'the reign of God' or 'the rule of God' and occasionally 'the realm of God'. To quote Hunter, 'the dominant meaning is always of God acting in His kingly power, exercising His sovereignty'.[5] Edersheim defines the Kingdom of God as, 'the rule of God which was manifested in and through Christ; is apparent in the Church; gradually develops amidst hindrances; is triumphant at the Second Coming of Christ (the end) and finally perfected in the world to come'.[6]

Fundamentally it is the rule of God established in the hearts of sinners, the answer to the prayer which Jesus taught us to pray, 'Thy Kingdom come; Thy will be done on earth as it is in heaven'. As Hunter points out, when Jesus came it was the reign of God breaking into history in order to visit and redeem His people. 'It is something which has not emerged from history,' says William Barclay, 'but which has invaded time out of eternity.'[7] 'In short,' quoting Hunter again, 'the eternal God was now laying bare His arm and signally manifesting His sovereignty in the Person and Work of Jesus.'[8]

Whereas the Kingdom is active in the present with a constant looking forward to its triumphant consummating, it is important and relevant to appreciate how wonderfully it is foreshadowed in former teaching. Edersheim declares, 'This rule of Heaven and kingship of Jehovah was the very substance of the Old Testament; the object of the calling and mission of Israel . . . Thus the whole of the Old Testament was the preparatory presentation of the rule of Heaven, and of the kingship of its Lord.'[9] It is implied in the protevangel (Gen. 3:15), and its manifestation on earth began with Abraham (Matt. 8:11; Lk. 13:28; Jn. 8:56). The coming of the Kingdom was indeed the common hope of Israel.

When Jesus came, therefore, His own announcement and the announcement of John the Baptist that the Kingdom of God was at hand had special significance for the Jewish race. While they looked forward to a fulfilment of the Kingdom with the coming of the Messiah, they believed that their racial link with Abraham provided them with an automatic membership of the Kingdom. This was very real indeed and something that could not be denied or ignored. Notice for example how Paul writes in Romans chapter 3, 'Then what advantage has the Jew? Or, what is the value of circumcision? Much in every way.' And he continues in chapter 9, 'They are Israelites, and to them *belong* the sonship, the glory, the covenants, the giving of the law, the worship and the promises; to them *belong* the patriarchs, and of their race, according to the flesh is the Christ.' Notice the use of the word 'belong'. This was undoubtedly in the mind of Nicodemus who came to Jesus by night and to whom Jesus declared, 'truly, truly, I say to you, unless one is born anew, he cannot see the Kingdom of God.' And again, 'Truly, truly, I say to you, unless one is born of water and the Spirit, he cannot enter the Kingdom of God.' Nicodemus was a devout and godly Pharisee, an accredited teacher in Israel. Quite rightly he thought of himself as one to whom the kingdom properly belonged, though in coming to Jesus as he did he indicated that he had already begun to realize his need of something more than a mere title or an automatic membership. On this memorable night he listened as Jesus spoke to him of something entirely new. The Master spoke of a truly spiritual membership of the kingdom made possible by the sovereign work of God manifested and by the power of the Holy Spirit which is entered into by a personal act of faith. This was the NEW BIRTH.

'We have the paradox,' says William Barclay, 'that the Kingdom is something which is given, and which is the direct result of the action of God, and yet at the same time is very much dependent upon the action and reaction of men.'[10] 'It is a divine act, not a divine demand,' says Hunter.[11] And Edersheim superbly declares, 'Every moral system is a road by which through self-denial, discipline and effort, men seek to reach a goal. Christ begins with this goal and places his disciples at once in the position to which all other teachers point at the end. They work up to the goal of becoming "children of the Kingdom". He makes men such, freely of His grace; and this *is* the Kingdom. What others labour for He gives. They begin by demanding, He by bestowing because He brings good tidings of forgiveness and mercy.'[12] (See Luke 12:32).

We may helpfully think of the Kingdom of God therefore as an inheritance. In fact it is spoken of as such in Matthew 25:34 and 1 Corinthians 6:9–10.

Previously it belonged especially and particularly to the Jews but under the new covenant it is now also for the possession of the Gentiles.

An inheritance is something that *belongs,* to a minor for example. By the time the age of discretion has arrived such an inheritance must be appreciated and understood and then appropriated and enjoyed. On the other hand it can be refused.

In this sense the kingdom belonged to Nicodemus and to all the members of the Jewish race. But only by the birth from above could they appreciate its true meaning and enter into it here and now, and in a fuller sense at the Second Coming of Christ.

So it is with children. Jesus spoke of the kingdom belonging to them. In their case, however, this was not for any reason of race or of possible Christian parent relationship, and certainly not because of childlike worthiness or coming to Jesus in repentance and faith in an adult-orientated way, it was only through God's grace and because of the atoning work of Christ.

In God's good time it is expected that they will acknowledge the reign and rule of God and possess the kingdom for themselves by the illumination and calling of the Holy Spirit and by the birth which is from above.

The responsibility Jesus has laid upon all of us who love him is to let the children come to Him and not hinder them. Not only those of our own families and in our churches, but also those who live in the neighbourhood and play in the streets. We hinder children by neglecting to be concerned and not caring enough. We do this by allowing their spiritual needs to be the concern of anyone but ourselves, and the result is we deny our time, our prayers and our money. We can only obey Christ's command to let them come by beginning to care for them.

It was the heartless and unspiritual behaviour of the disciples in rejecting the children and scolding their mothers that called for a rare demonstration of indignation on the part of Jesus. This was coupled with this solemn charge for which there needs to be a new awareness amongst Christian people everywhere – 'Let the children come to me, and do not hinder them; for to such belongs the Kingdom of Heaven'.

Because the Kingdom of Heaven belongs to children it is neither unreasonable nor illogical to allow that children also belong to the Kingdom. At this point I want to refer to Matthew 18 verses 1–14 which have been called 'The Children's Charter.' They certainly contain many key statements concerning the importance of children to God and their spiritual status prior to the age of responsibility.

It is important to note that the Greek word used for child is the same as in chapter 19:14 which, as we have already seen, can be applied to a boy or girl up to the age of 12. It is misleading to translate the word *little child* as in the Authorized Version and some modern translations of the Bible. The child who came when Jesus called him, and whom Jesus put in the midst, was at least old enough to be there without apparent adult supervision.

It is true that in verses 6, 10 and 14 Jesus uses the Greek word *mikros* which is translated *little one*.

I would like to believe that it was simply a beautiful word of endearment giving an insight into our Lord's tender love for children. I often find myself calling even a 9 or 10 year old 'my little one'; it is a lovely expression if used with the right tone of voice.

But in Matthew 18 it was also clearly used by our Lord as a comparison between the child in the midst and the adult disciples whose question he was answering.

Mikros has to do with size and not age; for example, '*little* flock' in Luke 12:32; then Zacchaeus was '*small* of stature' in Luke 19:3, whilst the tongue is a '*little* member' in James 3:5. This is also how we use the word in its English form. For example microbe, microfilm, microscope, and so on. All children in this sense are physically little when compared with the adults. The use of the words, 'little ones', therefore, does not limit what Jesus is so profoundly saying, to very young children. It is extremely important for us to remember that what is said may apply to any boy or girl before the age of accountability.

I am aware that some commentators regard 'little ones' in this passage as referring to a wider company than children, just as John addresses adult believers as 'my little children' (See 1 John 2:12–18 and 3:18). In this context, however, and viewing the passage as a whole, it would seem to be reasonable to allow these words of Jesus to refer directly to the children themselves.

Notice too that this was not a special child. It was just an ordinary boy or girl who happened to be there at the time. Undoubtedly it was a Jewish child but there is nothing nationalistic in the discourse to exclude the Gentile children who will eventually be contained in the proclamation of the Gospel. The child was not catechized, but was simply put in the midst, and whilst Jesus did not say it in so many words, the child or any child for that matter was Jesus' visual answer to the question which the disciples had asked: 'Who is the greatest in the kingdom of heaven?' By the action of our Lord, and by His teaching which followed, it must be perfectly clear that the child was considered by Him to be one who by nature was inside rather than outside the Kingdom.

Initially Jesus uses the child to teach the importance and example of childlike trust. It is worth noticing that He never points children to adults to be their examples but always adults to children (compare Matthew 21:15–16; Luke 18:17).

So, with the child in the midst, Jesus begins His teaching (v3), 'Truly I say to you, unless you turn and become like children, you will never enter the kingdom of heaven'.

Clearly from this first statement our Lord teaches that it is adults and not children who must convert or turn. Many children will have no experience of conversion in this biblical meaning of the word. From their earliest days, their attitude to the Saviour will have been one of response.

Secondly, Jesus said (v4), 'Whoever humbles himself like this child, he is the greatest in the kingdom of heaven'.

This takes us back to the original enquiry of the disciples, which has been the question of adults since the world began, 'Who is the greatest?'

Christ's answer was that the kingdom of heaven is as different from the ambitions and strivings and possessions of men in the world as a child's simplicity is different from an adult's aggressiveness. (See Romans 14:13–18 and 1 Corinthians 4:18–21).

Now comes the quite remarkable statement: 'Whoever receives one such child in my name receives me.' (v5). These moving words of our Lord should stir our hearts in practical concern for the spritual welfare of children. Do we wish to serve Christ and show our love and devotion to him? Then let us serve the children and show our love and devotion to them for Christ's sake. For receiving and loving children is receiving and loving Christ.

Words like these, 'Whoever receives one such child ... receives me', could not possibly be applied to a child who did not belong to the kingdom. Jesus said of all children that: 'their angels always behold the face of my Father who is in heaven' (v10), and again, 'See that you do not despise them' or as we might say in modern idiom 'Don't write them off'. Jesus then, deplored the kind of child discrimination of which we are so often guilty today. In Christ's eyes all children, whoever they are, are important to God, and all belong to His kingdom.

Matthew Henry comments, 'We must not look upon these little ones as contemptible, because really they are considerable; let not earth despise those whom heaven respects, nor let them be looked upon as with disdain, whom God has put honour upon, and looks upon with respect as his favourites.'

The angels Christ speaks of are the ministering spirits we read about in Hebrews 1:14 'sent forth to serve, for the sake of those who are to obtain salvation'. It should be clearly understood that these angels are not little children who have died, but the separate creation of God's myriad messengers. William Barclay calls them the 'liaison officers between God and man' and goes on to comment, 'The picture here is of a great royal court where only the most favoured courtiers and ministers and officials have direct access to the king. In the sight of God the children are so important that their guardian angels have always the right of direct access to the very presence of God Himself.'[13]

'Do not despise; do not look down upon a single one of these children', Jesus says, 'for their angels always behold the face of my Father.' They are important to God; they must be important to you. Do not dare to presume that this one is saved, and that one is not.

But we must now return to verse 6 in order to consider the terrible condemnation which is declared by our Lord towards anyone who causes a child to sin or to stumble. Jesus said, 'Whoever causes one of these little ones who believe in me to sin, it would be better for him to have a great millstone fastened round his neck and to be drowned in the depth of the sea.' (R.S.V.).

'To cause to sin' is *skandalise* in the Greek. It means putting an obstacle in someone's path. N.E.B. translates, '. . . if a man is a cause of stumbling to one of these little ones . . .' The New English Bible also puts verse 7 into the same paragraph as verses 5 and 6. (J. B. Phillips does the same) and translates, 'Alas for the world that such causes of stumbling arise: Come they must, but woe betide the man through whom they come.'

Here then is a solemn warning by our Lord to all Christian parents and to all of us who exercise responsibility in teaching, and caring for, children. A warning we need to remember more often.

Canon Stafford Wright has a helpful comment, 'Original sin is both individual and corporate. No child is born into the world in a neutral state. On the other hand no child is born into a Christianly mature family, and certainly not into a mature community. Thus the unfolding of its inner world is in an atmosphere which is to a greater or less extent polluted. Its fears, its desires for affection, its longing for freedom and yet to be under authority, its awareness of reward and punishment, all these longings are inadequately met by fallen parents and teachers often with the best will in the world'.[14]

So the responsibility of example and precept which our Lord lays upon all of us who are concerned with children cannot be too strongly emphasized. Using stirring metaphor and legitimate exaggeration, Jesus tells of the judgment awaiting those who cause offence and stumbling to a child. He speaks of a great millstone (big enough to need an ass to turn it round) being tied to their necks and their being thrown into the sea, suggesting complete oblivion.

There are some who look upon verses 8 to 9 as a repetition in parentheses of our Lord's teaching found in Matthew 5:30.

It is more consistent, however, to accept that the first fourteen verses of Matthew 18, in their entirety, apply to children. In verses 8 and 9 the Greek word translated 'to sin' is *skandalizo*. This means that the hands, eyes and feet of both parents and worker must be disciplined and dedicated if they are not to be a cause of offence.

Jesus ends this important discourse with the parable of the straying sheep.

Notice first the absence of verse 11 in all the reliable modern versions of the Bible including the Revised Version of 1881. The verse recorded in the Authorized Version says, 'For the Son of Man is come to save that which was lost', and is an interpolation in this passage. It is a statement of wonderful truth, of course, but properly belong to Luke 19:10 and the record of the adult Zacchaeus. The fact of the matter is that the sheep in the story, told when Jesus had a child in the midst, is not a *lost* sheep but a *straying* sheep. This is extremely important to remember.

Jesus sums it all up by declaring, 'So it is not the will of my Father in heaven that one of these little ones should perish'. J. B. Phillips translates even more forthrightly, 'You can understand then that it is never the will of your Father in heaven that a single one of these little ones should be lost.'

Our Lord's own teaching, therefore, concerning the spiritual state of the child is perfectly clear. It is possible that the child may have wandered and gone astray. He may even have been *led astray* by the behaviour of older people. But he is not lost – not yet. If he is properly loved, taught and prayed for, there is every reason to expect that, by the wonderful grace of God, he never will be lost.

It is because of these great statements of our Lord as recorded in chapters 18 and 19 of Matthew, and in the corresponding passages in Mark and Luke, that I am convinced that we must look upon *all children* as being included in the great atoning sacrifice of Calvary. They belong to Jesus Christ and to God until such time as they may deliberately refuse Him.

There are however spiritual privileges, that belong particularly to the children of Christian parents, and these must now engage our attention.

Chapter Three

SOME ARE MORE PRIVILEGED

All of us will agree that the boys and girls who are born to Christian parents cannot help but benefit from the training and environment that belong to a Christian home. These are the privileged children who are brought up in the 'nurture and admonition of the Lord', or, as the Revised Standard Version renders Ephesians 6:4, 'in the discipline and instruction of the Lord'.

There is an awareness of Christ in a home where everything is God-centred. These children are taught the meaning of right and wrong in an authoritative way. They are prayed for, and they constantly hear the name of Jesus lovingly and reverently pronounced. They hear the Scriptures read. They are taught to pray, and to read the Bible for themselves. They are taught to love the House of God which they probably attend together with their parents, and they will doubtless benefit from meeting and talking to other Christian people. Finally, they are taught to confess their 'sins' to one another, and to bring their failings and shortcomings regularly to the throne of God's grace for cleansing and forgiveness.

The meaning of the Christian festivals is carefully taught and happily remembered and there is a constant awareness of the promise of our Lord to come again.

In short the child who is fortunate to have informed and godly believing parents will be nurtured and trained as a Christian child throughout his growth and development. There will be no spiritual apartheid which shuts off any member as one who 'does not yet belong to Jesus'.

In support of this I am encouraged to discover that a

hundred years ago Horace Bushnell declared that the true idea of Christian training is that the child is to grow up a Christian and not know himself as being otherwise.[1] 'In other words', he continues, 'the aim, effort and expectation should be not, as is commonly assumed, that the child is to grow up in sin to be converted after he comes to a mature age; but that he is to open on to the world as one that is spiritually renewed, not remembering the time when he went through a technical experience, but seeming rather to have loved what is good from his earliest years.'

Bushnell goes on to plead that 'there is no absurdity in supposing that children are to grow up in Christ ... and if there is to be no absurdity there is a very clear moral incongruity in setting up a contrary supposition.'[2]

And again, 'So all human souls, the infantile as well as the adult have a nurture of the Spirit appropriate to their age and wants. What opinion is more essentially monstrous, in fact, than that which regards the Holy Spirit as having no agency in the immature souls of children who are growing up helpless and unconscious into the perils of time?'

Parents should realize that the home and family are but instruments in God's hand for the training of children in his ways. To accept this is to bring their children up as children of God. To nurture and train them through the years as Christians. It is a privileged responsibility.

In Psalm 68:6 we read that God puts the solitary into families, so that we may reverently say that the family is God's idea.[3] It is an organism, and this is true whether it is Christian or pagan. The universal character of the family is evidenced in Jeremiah 7:17–18 where the prophet declares 'Do you not see what they are doing in the cities of Judah, and in the streets of Jerusalem? The children gather wood, the fathers kindle fire, and the women knead dough, to make cakes for the queen of heaven.' This is the spontaneous working of a household together fashioning each other like stones in a brook. There is not only a physical likeness, but a likeness also in custom, mannerism, behaviour and outlook. Whatever fire the fathers may be kindling it is certain that the children will be gathering wood and the mother will be using this to fulfil her part in the combined family operation.

'The children fall into place naturally, as it were and unconsciously do and suffer what the scheme of the house requires,' Bushnell says, and continues: 'The godly home is to be the organic channel of Christian nurture to the growing child so that Christ himself, by that renewing Spirit who can sanctify from the womb, shall be practically infused into the child's mind; in other words that the home having a domestic spirit of grace dwelling in it, should become the church of childhood, the table and hearth of holy rite . . . the liveliness of a good life, the repose of faith, the confidence of righteous expectation, the sacred and cheerful liberty of the Spirit – all glowing about the young soul, as a warm and genial nurture and forging in it by methods that are silent and imperceptible, a spirit of duty and religious obedience to God. This only is Christian nurture. The nurture of the Lord.'

And again, from Bushnell, as already quoted in Chapter One, 'Understand that it is the family spirit, the organic life of the house, the silent power of a domestic godliness, working as it does unconsciously and with sovereign effect – this is it which forms your children to God. And if this be wanting all that you may do beside will be as likely to annoy and harden as to bless.'[4]

A contemporary and colleague of George Whitfield wrote, 'Every Christian family ought to be, as it were, a little church, consecrated to Christ and wholly influenced and governed by His rules. And family education and order are some of the chief means of grace. If these fail, all other means are likely to prove ineffectual.'[5]

There follows naturally from this awareness of the organic unity and influence of a godly home the reasonableness of regeneration for the children of parents who love the Lord.

Horace Bushnell puts it like this, '. . . it is the privilege and duty of every Christian parent that his children shall come forth into action as a regenerate stock. The organic unity is to be a power of life. God engages on His part that it may be, and calls the Christian parent to promise on his part that it shall be.'[6]

If there should be some who might think that this is going too far, it is helpful to notice what Bushnell also says, 'So if there be an organic power of character in the parent, such as that of which I have spoken, it is not a complete power in itself but only such a power as demands the realizing presence of the Spirit of God, both to the parent and to the child to give it effect.'[7]

It has become my growing conviction over the years that godly believing parents should prayerfully expect that this sovereign work of regeneration will be a happening in the lives of their children at a very early stage, and that it is reasonable to agree with Bushnell when he says that 'God engages on His part that it may be, and calls the Christian parent to promise on his part that it shall be.' This quite apart from the practice or non-practice of infant or household baptism. I base this conviction on what is written in the Scriptures concerning Jeremiah and John the Baptist.

This was the 'word of the Lord' to Jeremiah, 'Before I formed you; I appointed you a prophet to the nations.' (Jer. 1:4–5).

And this was the word of the angel of the Lord to Zacharias concerning John, 'And you will have joy and gladness, and many will rejoice at his birth; for he will be great before the Lord, and he shall drink no wine nor strong drink, and he will be filled with the Holy Spirit even from his mother's womb.' (Luke 1:14–15)

These were ordinary human children, and the fact that the Holy Spirit was at work in their lives even before they were born reveals at once that such a happening is completely and reasonably within the scope and intention of providence. We may also profitably compare the spiritual progress of the child Samuel, with whom I have dealt in Chapter One, and recall that he was 'in favour with the Lord' before he was able to make his own intelligent response. These Scriptural examples should encourage us to believe that the new life of God may be planted in the hearts of children at a very early moment in their lives, or even before they are born.

My conviction that infant regeneration is a reasonable thing is also based upon the evidence I constantly see in the lives of both younger and older children.

Let me make this clear.

All too often the thing that is spoken of is the evidence of original sin in the lives of all children. Even in the behaviour patterns of the children of Christian parents we notice selfishness, greed, temper, disobedience and so on. We allow these things to hide from us their very real love for the Saviour and their acts of devotion, kindness and love. We also confuse 'naughtiness', often caused by tiredness, frustration and parental unreasonableness, with wilful sinfulness and rebellion, forgetting that self-control, the fruit of the Spirit, is often slow in growing, and needs much parental patience and training. We ignore the sad fact that there are inconsistencies in our own lives too. If we are sensitive to the love and the holiness of God, we shall find ourselves crying out, 'O wretched man that I am!' Our consolation is that in spite of our own mixed behaviour, we know that we do love the Lord. As the Anglican Article expresses it, 'the infection of original or birth sin remaineth even in them that are regenerate.'[8] We must therefore not be surprised to discover that what is true in our own Christian experience is also evident in the lives of our children. Their similar mixed behaviour which they are not as yet so skilled in hiding as their parents, does not necessarily mean that they are not yet regenerate.

Growing up with a Christian father and mother or perhaps just one Christian parent, these children learn to love the Lord from their earliest days.

When enjoying the hospitality of Christian homes I have constantly seen the desire of these children to please Christ in a way that puts older folk to shame. This, I maintain is true evidence of the life of God implanted in their young hearts.

The regeneration of infants then is a reasonable happening and this New Birth, whenever it takes place, is the unconditional and sovereign work of God. Our Lord made this perfectly clear when He said to Nicodemus, 'The wind blows where it wills, and you hear the sound of it, but you do not know whence it comes, or whither it goes; so it is with every one who is born of the Spirit.' (John 3:8)

While it is often true in the case of adults, and of children from non-Christian homes, that conversion and regeneration coincide in time, we must beware of saying that when the individual converts, God regenerates. We shall see that the proper thing to say is that when God regenerates the individual is able to convert. God always takes the initiative. It is a birth *from above*.

'So do not be deceived my beloved brethren. Every good endowment and every perfect gift is from above, coming down from the Father of lights with whom there is no variation or shadow of change. Of his own will he brought us forth (he gave us birth – New English Bible) by the word of truth that we should be a kind of firstfruits of his creatures.' (James 1:16–18)

Bishop Ryle wrote long ago, 'The change is one which no man can give to himself, nor yet to another. It would be as reasonable to expect the dead to raise themselves, or to require an artist to give a marble statue life. The children of God are born not of blood, nor of the will of the flesh, but of God.'[9]

While then it is sometimes true that the outcome of the activity of the Holy Spirit will issue in a coincidental happening of regeneration on God's part and conversion, or turning and trusting, on the part of the individual, in the case of a child whose parents are believers we may legitimately expect that the life of God will be implanted many years before it is understood or appreciated. At the same time its effects will be manifested in the life and behaviour of the child during the years that anticipate his conscious experience of personal faith and trust in the Saviour.

In this context notice what A. A. Hodge had to say a hundred years ago about conversion and regeneration. 'Conversion signifies the first exercise of the new disposition

4

implanted in regeneration; i.e. in freely turning to God. Regeneration is God's act; conversion is ours. Regeneration is the implanting of a gracious principle; conversion is the exercise of the principle. Regeneration is never a matter of direct consciousness to the subject of it; conversion always is such to the agent of it. Regeneration is a single act, complete in itself, and never repeated; conversion as the beginning of holy living is the commencement of a series, constant, endless, and progressive.'[10] It is misleading, therefore, to believe that an experience of conversion is a requisite of regeneration, while it is equally wrong to declare, 'You must be born again', with the implication that the individual who is addressed has a responsibility to bring about or ensure its happening.

It is also misleading to insist, as some do, on a stereotyped pattern of response from any individual, let alone a child, in his experience of regeneration. I quote again from Horace Bushnell, 'Many true Christians . . . make a merit of great persistency and firmness in asserting the universal necessity of a new spiritual birth; not perceiving under what varieties of form that change may be wrought. The soul must be exercised, they think, in one given way, *viz.* by a struggle with sin, a conscious self renunciation, and a true turning to Christ for mercy, followed by the joy and peace of a new life in the Spirit. A child, in other words, can be born to God only in the same way as an adult can be. There is no quickening grace, or new creation, of the Spirit, proper to him as a child. If he dies in infancy, God may, it is true, find some way possibly to save him, but if he stays among the living, he cannot be a Christian until he is older. He is therefore left in this most beautiful and pliant age in a condition most of all unprivileged, and most sadly unhopeful. The necessity of a great spiritual change is upon him, and yet he is wholly incapable of the change.'[11]

When we turn to the Scriptures, however, we discover an amazingly wide variety even in the pattern of adult response and the experience of spiritual blessing of those who were evidently born again by the Spirit. The classic examples are Paul on the Damascus Road, and the gaoler at Philippi, both dramatic and critical and in contrast to the experience of Lydia 'whose heart the Lord opened'.

Lydia's response was the kind which has been likened to the gradual opening of a flower to the sun. It was the kind of experience which belonged to young Campbell Morgan quoted in Chapter One – '. . . so that when the necessity came for my personal choosing, so did I recognize the claims of His love, that without revulsion, and hardly knowing when, I yielded to Him my allegiance and my love.'

This is the ideal way for any child to come to the Saviour, and it is likely to be the normal experience of children of believing parents who 'give their children to Christ and never doubting their acceptance by him, do train them as his.'

This was my own experience during a rampageous childhood. I made a conscious and very real response to the Saviour at the age of seven, at the close of a week-night children's service, though I cannot remember the time when I did not love him. It also became true in different ways and at different ages for all my brothers and sisters in my own Christian Brethren home.

For all these reasons, therefore, I am persuaded that 'the new life is often planted in the hearts of children of Christian families at a very early moment in their lives, and long before the age of discretion and accountability.' The unity of the Christian family will be found to be a power of life to the child as the Spirit of God is present to give it effect both to parent and child.[12]

Closely linked to the expectation of regeneration and its privileges for the children of Christian parents, is the important doctrine of 'Covenant Relationship'.

At the moment of the Fall, and in the context of judgment, God announced to Adam and Eve that it was His will to rescue man from ruin, and to give him justification and life. The promise of God which we call the Protevangel, that the seed of the woman should bruise the serpent's head, was his immediate provision for the sin of our first parents, and also for their posterity. This was the covenant of God's grace. It was repeated to Noah, and crystallized to Abraham when God said, 'And I will establish my covenant between me and you and your descendants after you, throughout their generations for an everlasting covenant, to be God to you and to your descendants after you.' *I will be your God and you shall be my people'* (Genesis 17:7; Leviticus 26:12; Jeremiah 11:4; 30:22)

For the purpose of its accomplishment by Christ, the covenant was temporarily confined to the Jewish race (see Romans 9:4–5) though members of other nations were not excluded. By faith in Jehovah as the only true God, by a promise of obedience and by submission to the rite of circumcision (the seal of the covenant) the true proselyte could occupy a place in the Church and nation of Israel, equal to that of a son or daughter in the natural line of descent. So Abraham was instructed to circumcize, as a sign and seal of the covenant, not only those who were born in his house, but also foreigners who had been bought with his money. (Genesis 17:12–13) In the New Testament, even before our Lord had died and risen again to make possible the fulfilment of the covenant promises, it was declared, almost certainly by Christ Himself, that 'God so loved the world that He gave His only Son, that *whosoever* believes in Him should not perish but have eternal life.' This is the Good News of God which is nothing other than the 'Covenant of Grace.'[13] It is declared to be a New Covenant. Its newness is found in its being, now manifestly, as it was always purposefully, centered in Christ. It is now more concerned with spiritual than material or temporal blessing although these still belong to the promises. Also it is now more than ever before extended to all nations. In essence, however, it is the renewal of the original promise to believing men and women and their posterity, 'I will be your God and you shall be my people.'[14][15]

So we find Peter concluding his sermon on the Day of Pentecost with these words, 'Repent, and be baptized every one of you in the name of Jesus Christ for the forgiveness of

your sins; and you shall receive the gift of the Holy Spirit.'
'For the promise is to you and to your children and to all that
are far off, every one whom the Lord our God calls to Him.'
(Acts 2:38–39)

The fulfilment of the covenant and its proclamation to
pagans is by the preaching of the word of God. Its blessings
are also conveyed through the influence of Christian living
and through the prayerful concern of the Christian for his
relatives, neighbours and friends. In the Old Testament 'the
Lord blessed the Egyptian's house for Joseph's sake'.
(Genesis 39:5) and in the New Testament a paralytic man
was blessed by Jesus because a group of his friends was
concerned for his well being (Mark 2:1–12). Mary and
Martha were the means of blessing for Lazarus, their brother
(John 11). In the same way there are today godly leaders and
teachers who are the means of bringing the blessings of the
'Covenant of Grace' to the children of non-Christian or
nominally Christian homes. They are dedicated men and
women who give their lives in response to Christ's request to
let the children come to him.

But it is the children who belong to Christian homes, who
are likely to be fortunate in the experimental enjoyment and
appropriation of the blessings which belong to the 'Covenant
of Grace'. Unfortunately, far too many Christian parents
have never quite appreciated the spiritual responsibility which
God has given to them, or the spiritual potential with which
God has entrusted them for the blessing of their children.
Consequently they are not as concerned as they should be in
fulfilling the conditions upon which the blessings of the
covenant to their own children must largely depend. These are
not automatic blessings for the children of believers. They are
the promises of God, to be desired, taught, and prayerfully
appropriated by godly parents on behalf of their own
children. For it is in the economy of God and clearly taught
in both the Old and New Testaments that these blessings of
the covenant are to be conveyed primarily to sons and
daughters through believing parents in the environment of the
home, and through the organism of the family. Parents

therefore who all too easily bewail the absence of spiritual response in their own children, must remember that the responsibility for this is one which cannot be shifted on to the child, or relegated to any outside influence. In God's sight and intention it is a responsibility which belongs primarily to the parents themselves.

Constantly in the Old Testament, in the context of covenant teaching, parents are encouraged to believe that their children are included with themselves in the promises. It is their business to be active in spiritual relationships with their sons and daughters, by example and faith, instruction and prayer.

The following examples from the Bible illustrate the God-given responsibility which is to be exercised by present-day Christian parents towards their own children, and the duty which belongs particularly to the father of the family.

Noah

We turn first to Genesis 7:1, 'Then the Lord said to Noah, "Go into the ark, *you and all your household,* for I have seen that you are righteous before me in this generation."' Compare the New Testament passage from Hebrews 11:7, 'By faith Noah . . . took heed and constructed an ark for *the saving of his household.*'

Abraham

We have already noticed that it was with Abraham that God established His covenant. The declaration of Jehovah recorded in Genesis 17 cannot be too strongly emphasized: 'And I will establish my covenant between me and you and your descendants after you, throughout their generations for an everlasting covenant, to be God to you and to your descendants after you.'

Notice particularly here that it is *an everlasting covenant* and notice also the remarkable appropriation by Paul in his letter to the Galatians, of its validity, and relevance for present-day parents and children, 'And if you are Christ's, then you are Abraham's offspring, heirs according to promise' (Gal. 3:29).

Again, in his letter to the Romans, 'This means that it is not the children of the flesh who are the children of God, but the children of the promise are reckoned as descendants.' (Rom. 9:8)

'Such was the promise given to Abraham,' says Andrew Murray, 'Such is the promise for every believing parent.'[16]

Moses

The Epistle to the Hebrews (11:23) tells us that 'By faith Moses, when he was born, was hid for three months by his parents because they saw that the child was beautiful; and they were not afraid of the king's edict.' Exodus 2:1–3 provides us with the Old Testament description of the event. 'And when (Jochebed, the mother of Moses) saw that he was a goodly child, she hid him three months. And when she could hide him no longer she took for him a basket made of bulrushes, and daubed it with bitumen and pitch; and she put the child in it and placed it among the reeds on the river's brink.'

I quote Andrew Murray again, 'And so the eye of faith sees in each little one a Divine goodliness, and hides it in the shadow of the Almighty. Is it not an object of the great Redemption; destined to be a partaker of the precious blood and the Holy Spirit of Jesus? So let it be a settled thing with thy heart that he has accepted thy trust ... and cannot disappoint thy faith.'[17] 'And when the time comes that he must come into contact with the world, commit thy child boldly to the waters in the ark of the covenant of thy God.'[18]

There is neither time nor space to consider all the Old Testament references to children in the context of the family. There are the instructions concerning the Passover in

Exodus 12, when the lamb was taken by the father, and its blood sprinkled by faith on behalf of the household, and especially of the eldest son. The sanctification of the first-born in Exodus 13: the keeping of the Sabbath in Exodus 20: the children's commandment in Exodus 20, carried forward to be an important part of the instruction and discipline of boys and girls in the New Testament church in Ephesians 6:1 and Colossians 3:20: the magnificent passage in Deuteronomy 6:1–7 concerning the responsibility of parents, and particularly fathers, to teach the Scriptures to their own children in the home.

Notice in 1 Kings 17 how Elijah prayed for the orphan boy at Zarephath and identified himself with someone else's child. Recall the experience of Hannah in the early chapters of 1 Samuel, and echo her cry to God, 'For this child I prayed; and the Lord has granted me my petition which I made to Him. Therefore I have lent him to the Lord.' We can look forward, as Hannah undoubtedly did, to the day when our own child will, like Samuel, grow up with the Lord and say for himself, 'Speak for your servant hears.'

The covenant references to children and parents in the Old Testament would seem to be endless. We must content ourselves here with this brief analysis and say with Joshua, 'As for me *and my house* we will serve the Lord.' (Joshua 24:15)

In the Gospels, as in the Acts and the Epistles we find, as we should expect, that the teaching and action of our Lord himself and of his followers are in harmony with the concepts of the Old Testament concerning the spiritual unity of the family and its importance as a conveyance for the promises of God.

Marcel's words already quoted in Chapter One are also relevant here, 'In God's eyes parents and their children are one. By divine right parents are the authorized representatives of their children: they act for them; they engage in spiritual obligations because of them, and also in their name. Such is the order of God.'[19] And he goes on to quote from a writing of R. Mehl, 'Thanks to individualism and to philosophical idealism, we have ceased to consider the family as a spiritual reality, forgetting that Jesus regarded it as a unitary whole before God and that He performed His miracles for such a child or such a servant because of the faith alone of the father of the family.'[20]

So we find Jesus blessing the nobleman's son (John 4) – and Jairus's daughter (Mark 5), and the paralytic boy (Mark 9), all by the faith and importunity of their parents.

Constantly in the New Testament we discover that the household and family is included in the blessing of salvation which has been experienced by a father or mother. Examples: Zacchaeus (Luke 19); the nobleman (John 4); and Onesiphorus (2 Timothy 1:16): the Philippian gaoler (Acts 16).

It is also interesting to recall Paul's significant words to Timothy in his second letter to him, 'I am reminded of your sincere faith. A faith that dwelt first in your grandmother Lois and your mother Eunice and now, I am sure, dwells in you.' This is a divine progression – grandmother Lois – mother Eunice – son Timothy. It is a pattern which occurs over and over again.

Marcel also points out that the influence of the covenant will affect everything that is connected with the individual who has embraced it.[21] Not only will it affect his posterity, but also his money, his goods, his influence and authority, his job and his relationships, his intelligence and his heart, his science and his art, his social and political life. This means that there is a wide influence for good in a godly Christian home even if only one of the parents is a practising Christian. This is the most likely and satisfactory meaning of the controversial statement of Paul in his letter to Corinth, 'For the unbelieving husband is consecrated through his wife, and the unbelieving wife is consecrated through her husband. Otherwise your children would be unclean, but as it is they are holy.' (1 Cor. 7:14)

The Greek words for holy and consecrated have the same root meaning. It is important not to read into this declaration, which is a part of Paul's statement about mixed marriages, more than is intended. The child who is not yet old enough to say yes or no to the promise of the covenant for himself is no more and no less holy, than the unbelieving mother or father who in verse 16 is declared to be still unsaved. This does not however affect the status of the child of belonging to the Kingdom and being an inheritor of the promises.

In the New English Bible the translation of this admittedly difficult verse is a helpful one, 'For the heathen husband now belongs to God through his Christian wife, and the heathen wife through her Christian husband. Otherwise your children would not belong to God, whereas in fact they do.' But, as we have already seen, the status of belonging must be ratified sooner or later by the individual himself. The unbelieving husband may decide to say no, and subsequently, when he is old enough, so may the child. In this connection Marcel quotes Cullmann as follows, 'The possession by a child of Christian parentage is no guarantee of subsequent faith, but a divine indication of its probability.'[22]

In this context we must remember the teaching of Jesus in Matthew chapter ten which tells of the divisive propensity of the gospel in the home. There may be division because of him, for a man's bitterest foes may be those of his own household. Again Paul teaches in 1 Corinthians 7 quite realistically, that the home may be divided as a result of parents separating. We may hope however that these will be the exception rather than the rule, especially where both parents love the Lord.

It is important always to remember that it is the *promises* which are inherited by the child for the sake of its godly parents. The child does not inherit eternal life. Salvation itself is not hereditary.

The promises, however, are inherited by the children and we must include all the promises and not simply those concerning forgiveness and spiritual relationships. There are the promises concerning, election, the Christian calling, faith and the birth from above. All these are sovereign gifts, born of God's amazing grace and without which there can be no lasting blessing or real experience of enjoying and participating in the 'Covenant of Grace'.

Husband and wife, as a believing man and a believing woman, before ever their children are conceived, embrace the blessings of the covenant for themselves, and enter by faith into this precious relationship with God in the establishment of a home and the anticipation of a family. Their children before birth are entrusted to God. From the moment of their birth they are regarded as belonging to him. These parents look to God in faith for the fulfilment to their sons and daughters of all the promises which belong to this 'Covenant of Grace'. By godly example and teaching they will accept the responsibility of bringing up their own children in the nurture, discipline and instruction of the Lord. They will tell them of 'the glorious deeds of the Lord, and His might and the wonders which He has wrought.' (Psalm 78:4) They will look forward to the day when the children will embrace intelligently the promises for themselves, entering into covenant relationship with the Lord; when 'they will set their hope in God, and not forget the works of God, but keep His commandments.' (Psalm 78:7)

Parents will also follow the example of Abraham and exercise the same faith, not only for the children born in their families, but also for children who may have been adopted or who are being fostered. (See Genesis 17:9–13) The same kind of faith may also be exercised by all of us who love the Lord towards the children of unbelieving friends and neighbours whom we hope to gather into the family of our church, ideally with their parents. It is not sufficiently realized that God does bless children from non-Christian homes for the sake of those who are dedicated to the role of spiritual parent-substitutes on their behalf. These are men and women who are prepared to pray and care, and to become identified and involved, as well as to teach. They may be godly Sunday school teachers or Bible Class leaders or godparents. Equally they could be doctors or nurses; often they are day school teachers or social workers, ministers or evangelists.

These then are the blessings and privileges which are the heritage of all children who are fortunate enough to have Christian parents, or even Christian substitute parents:

1. The happiness and benefit for the child of being virtuously brought up in the nurture and admonition of the Lord, and of being treated as a Christian child throughout all the growing years.

2. The expectation that the life of God will be implanted in the heart of the child at a very tender age.

3. The inheritance for the child of all the promises that belong to the 'Covenant of Grace'.

4. The expectation that there will be a conscious and intelligent appropriation of all these things by the child in God's own time. This in all probability will be before the child leaves the Junior school at 11.

The Scriptures make it perfectly clear that these spiritual blessings are to be channelled to the children by the parents day by day in the home, through their instinctive and purposeful activity. This is not the impossible dream of an armchair writer. It is neither unrealistic nor impractical. The advice given in Ephesians chapter 6, concerning the upbringing of children, is not simply the counsel of an apostle, but the commandment of God. We expose both ourselves and our posterity to spiritual risk if we disobey.

My plea is not for an outdated programme of unreasonable Victorian restriction, but for consistant Christian living in the home. For lives that are Christ-like, gay, exciting, projective and sensible. For a quality of unified activity in the home, that will make these privileges real and meaningful to every Christian family.

Happy indeed is the home where the children are treated both by parents and each other as belonging to the Lord. Happy are the parents whose faith enables them to believe that the Lord will implant His own new life in the hearts of their little ones. It is beautiful to see the conscious personal response and appropriation by such children of the blessings of salvation through the effectual calling of God when the years of proper understanding are reached.

However in order to be realistic it must be admitted that there are children of Christian families who have grown up refusing the faith of their fathers, and this must be considered in a separate chapter.

First we must spare some thought for the large number of children who are spiritually under-privileged as a result of not having even one parent as a practising Christian.

Chapter Four

THE UNDERPRIVILEGED CHILD

Children who belong to non-Christian or nominal Christian families are every bit as important to God as the boys and girls whose parents are believers. They are all included in the statement of our Lord that 'to such belongs the Kingdom of Heaven' and, if we are able to accept the propositions I made in Chapter One, we shall agree that these children are covered by the great atoning sacrifice of Calvary, and belong to Christ until such time as they may say no, to him. Saying no to God and to Jesus may be by deliberate refusal, by materialistic indifference, by godless preoccupation, or by any of the other conscious or unconscious ways of rejection as described in the early chapters of Paul's letter to the Romans. In the end it adds up to 'loving the darkness rather than the light because their deeds are evil'. Many children from non-Christian homes are copying the godless and materialistic attitudes of parents and older brothers and sisters, and are saying no to God and his ways at a younger age than ever before.

Once again we have the unified pattern of a family, but this time it is a godless family. In its activity there is a real and constant projection of Jeremiah 7:17-19, quoted in Chapter Three: 'Do you not see what they are doing in the cities of Judah and in the streets of Jerusalem? The children gather wood, the fathers kindle fire, and the women knead dough, to make cakes for the queen of heaven; and they pour out drink offerings to other gods, to provoke me to anger. Is it I whom they provoke? says the Lord. Is it not themselves to their own confusion?'

In this twentieth century the *other gods* are materialism and humanism. The consequent confusion unavoidably embraces every member of the godless home.

This state of things commands our prayerful concern for all the children around us who are spiritually underprivileged by belonging to this kind of non-Christian or nominal Christian family. These children have few of the advantages described in Chapter Three as belonging to the sons and daughters of believing parents.

'No one is so poor as he for whom not a single soul is praying, he who has no one to take him personally and persistently to God in prayer,' says Hallesby.[1] Yet this is the pitiable state of millions of children whose parents have little or no time for God. No one ever prays for these boys and girls. Many of them hear the name of Jesus, or Christ, only in blasphemy. Many of them have a desire to pray but do not know how. They may know something of worship and something of the Scriptures from religious instruction in day school. The more fortunate ones have dedicated Christian day-school teachers who are concerned for their spiritual care and upbringing. A small proportion of these children also benefit from the teaching and care of our churches. The great majority of them, however, are spiritually impoverished. They get little or no spiritual help from their parents. They are certainly included in the promises of the 'Covenant of Grace', yet they are unaware of this. These are the 'outreach' children. They are spiritually deprived. We must minister to them in this sphere, as for example, a social worker would materially care for socially deprived children. We must gather them into our homes and churches, not only to 'get them saved' or to teach them the Bible, but also to be their spiritual parent substitutes.

Here are some of the ways in which our responsibilities towards these spiritually deprived children may be fulfilled:

1. Every child on the church register, as well as those on the cradle roll and others who may only be visited, must be prayed for every day. This is an undertaking for which I always plead when I visit a church for a children's mission.

2. The children must be taught to say their prayers meaningfully for themselves. I was made aware of this need many years ago when a shabby undersized boy of nine or ten in a depressed part of London said to me during a mission, 'Please, sir, I don't know how to say my prayers.' Nowadays this important piece of caring always forms a part of our children's weeks. We have printed a special 'Tell the Children How to Pray' card for the purpose.[2]

3. Boys and girls must not only be told that it is important to read the Bible for themselves, but shown how to do so, and encouraged to continue.

4. Positive moral teaching, and encouragement in the realms of reading and music and spare-time activities, will need to form a part of the caring programme for a surprisingly large proportion of these children.

5. It is important for these boys and girls to have the opportunity from time to time to engage in activities with Christian adults and their children, ideally in the setting of a Christian home.

6. The value to a child's character of training with other Christian boys and girls in some residential activity must be fully realized as indeed it now is by educational experts. In Somerset, for example, the aim is for every child to enjoy this kind of recreation, both in Junior and Secondary school. Years ago dedicated men and women pioneered the Christian houseparty and holiday camp and these have been greatly blessed by God. It should now be our aim for every child to enjoy at least a week of this specialized activity. The idea being to allow a child to enjoy a Christian environment amongst Christian helpers rather than being subjected to intensive evangelism. This also is caring.

7. Every child, through a church based mission, or similar evangelical effort, should have the opportunity to make a personal and positive response to the Saviour and this without undue pressure. The mission catering particularly for the children who already have a background of Bible teaching will be easily distinguished from the popular holiday club weeks which although equally valuable are rather more

of a free for all. Many churches I have visited arrange a three-year cycle of this more specialized teaching mission giving every child two opportunities of attending between the ages of eight and twelve.

8. During the growing-up years, responsible, intelligent membership of the local church will be encouraged by the care and prayer of the spiritual parent-substitute. This will be lovingly maintained and intensified by an increased measure of patience and sympathy. All these things will form part of spiritual caring, with parent liaison. The object in mind being to reach the whole family through the children and so establish another truly Christian home.

These should be spontaneous procedures on the part of the Christian worker, activated by the compulsive love of Jesus. He will be acting towards the child on behalf of defaulting parents in a wide variety of differing situations. There can be no list of rules. Even the caring list I have given is far from being exhaustive and will need to be used as a guide rather than a schedule of 'You must do this,'or 'You must do that.'

One of the difficult-to-understand, and difficult-to-accept Bible statements, which must be considered in any study of children who are spiritually deprived, occurs no less than four times in the Old Testament, and has its counterpart in the New (Exodus 20:5; 34:7; Numbers 14:18; Deuteronomy 5:9; Galatians 6:7-8). It is the declaration by Jehovah himself that the iniquities of the fathers are to be visited upon the children. There is no vindictiveness in this statement. It is made in the context of a magnificent declaration of the mercy and grace of God.

Here is the statement, as it is recorded in Exodus chapter 34: 'And the Lord descended in the cloud and stood with (Moses) there, and proclaimed the name of the Lord. The Lord passed before him and proclaimed. "The Lord, the Lord, a God merciful and gracious, slow to anger, and abounding in steadfast love and faithfulness, keeping steadfast

5

love for thousands, forgiving iniquity and transgression and sin, but who will by no means clear the guilty, visiting the iniquity of the fathers upon the children, and the children's children, to the third and fourth generation." '

As we seek to evaluate the significance of this scripture and its application specifically to children today, particularly those who belong to non-Christian families, there are three things to notice. First the statement is made with this background declaration of God's mercy and grace, his slowness to anger, his abounding in steadfast love, and his readiness to forgive. Secondly, it is made in the setting of the giving of the law on Mount Sinai. There is undoubtedly a special reference here to the iniquity of the father with regard to idolatry. The statement is fulfilled as the children are taken into captivity. Thirdly, there are parallel statements in Deuteronomy and Ezekiel concerning the sins of the fathers in relation to their children which bring the whole matter into perspective. Deuteronomy 24:16 says 'The fathers shall not be put to death for the children, nor shall the children be put to death for the fathers; every man shall be put to death for his own sin.' And Ezekiel 18:20, 'The soul that sins shall die. The son shall not suffer for the iniquity of the father, nor the father suffer for the iniquity of the son; the righteousness of the righteous shall be upon himself, and the wickedness of the wicked shall be upon himself.'

Compare Romans 2:6-8. This means that ultimately the wickedness of every individual must be upon himself – every man will be finally condemned for his own sin, his conscious or unconscious rejection of the mercy and grace of God in the person of Jesus Christ. The important and relevant principle, which becomes immediately evident, is that, whilst the child is clearly not to suffer the *penalties* of the parent's wrongdoing, he cannot help but be affected by the *consequences*.

While it is in the nature of fire to burn and of water to drench, so it is in the nature of goodness to bring benefit, and of iniquity to make desolate.

'Do not be deceived,' says Paul, 'God is not mocked, for whatever a man sows that he will also reap.' (Galatians 6:7-8)

Such reaping must by its very effect involve our friends and families in good or ill, especially the children.

It is significant to realize that some consider the industrial unrest of our age to be the working out of this principle of sowing and reaping. We are now reaping what others have sown. Our fathers and grandfathers were prepared to limit the 'good life' to the few. They condoned and perpetuated the wretched conditions of the industrial revolution, when women as well as men worked sixteen hours a day for a pittance, and child labour was eagerly sought for the mines and the factories. The present aggressiveness of 'black power' today towards the west is another example of the iniquities of the fathers coming upon the children. The act of the abolition of slavery brought by Wilberforce did not become law until as recently as 1833. A hundred and fifty years ago our fathers were still involved in the traffic of slaves. The consequences of this are now being visited upon the third and fourth generation. It might well be that the rigid adherence of some parents in the past to the traditional patterns (as distinct from the unchanging standards) of behaviour and fashion, is partly responsible for the rebellion against church and establishment by many of our younger generation.

Whilst these things might illustrate the wider outworkings of the principle, we are particularly concerned with the disadvantages brought to children by their parents' wrongdoings.

A parent's failure to write a note, pay a bill, fill up a form, keep an appointment or even get up in the morning can cause suffering to a child. It may only be trivial or of a temporary nature, nevertheless the child suffers in consequence. But there is much more serious suffering.

There are children physically diseased because of their parents' sexual promiscuousness. Others are suffering poverty because their parents are prodigal, extravagant, or lazy. Some are insecure, and have become anti-social because of their parents' infidelity. Many boys and girls are ignorant simply because of the lack of conversation in the home. At the other end of the social scale, there are many children who are completely godless and materialistic because of their wealthy parents' humanistic commitment to getting and spending. These are but a few of the more serious results of the iniquities of the fathers affecting the children. They are usually the lot of the children of non-Christian homes, though many of them have their counterparts in the sons and daughters of Christian parents. This principle of sowing and reaping, or cause and effect, though it can be overruled by the grace of God, will always be impartial in its consequential destiny. The gravest thing is that children from godless homes are often godless too because they are reaping the consequences of their parents' refusal to acknowledge and honour God.

Before leaving this study of children who are spiritually underprivileged it must be appreciated that many non-regular-churchgoing families are by no means completely godless. They are often happily integrated and disciplined with a tradition of upright behaviour and an ingrained awareness of The Almighty, this being the title they use for God. They are often pleasant, helpful, cultured people with a quiet, uninformed, rarely talked about, but nevertheless sincere faith. Once a month or so, they are found at an early service of Holy Communion. Usually a service without a sermon! Those who are not so affluent are likely to possess a much less sophisticated belief in God verging on the superstitious. They like to listen to the hymn singing on the radio or television, they admire and respect the Salvation Army, and they often become extremely sentimental in their observance of Christmas.

In between these two social extremes there are many shades of religious acknowledgment. The Christian situation in our own land is far from being a happy one but it must not be forgotten that there are still many non-church-going families who are by no means anti-God, and we must hesitate before writing them all off as complete outsiders.

It is the children from these homes who are most likely to come to our churches and Sunday schools. They may be expected to respect the teaching and to be well behaved. We must see to it that our own standards of presentation and discipline are all that they should be. We must constantly remember that these, often very attractive children from good homes, are also those who are spiritually underprivileged because most if not all of the ingredients that belong to a truly Christian home are lacking in their family upbringing. They will need spiritual care as well as teaching every bit as much as the children who come to us from the unruly and completely godless families.

All these spiritually underprivileged children are precious and important to God. Whether they come from godless and materialistic homes or from respectable integrated families. We have been commissioned by our Lord Himself to let them come to Him.

In Chapter One attention was drawn to these words which were spoken by our Lord, 'Whoever receives one such child in my name receives me.' The comment there is also relevant here. Do we wish to serve Christ and show our love to Him? Then let us serve the children and show our love to them.

Just over a hundred years ago children were expected to be seen and not heard. 'Speak when you're spoken to; do as you're bid; and shut the door after you there's a good kid.'

There were virtually no children's stories or suitable children's songs and hymns, and there were very few children's games. Not every child went to school. Many could neither read nor write. There were no children's services in our churches, and no proper orphanages or children's hospitals. Then it all seemed to happen at once – Lord Shaftesbury, Charles Dickens, Dr Barnardo, George Muller, Mrs Alexander, Lewis Carol, Beatrix Potter and last but by no means least, T. B. Bishop, Josiah Spiers and the Children's Special Service Mission. Children had suddenly become important. More recently, and almost certainly because of the unacceptability of the traditional adult-orientated approach, the spiritual aspect of the vision regarding children has become blurred. Teenagers are commanding much more of the time and concern of the churches and the societies than younger children. These must become important again in our spiritual concern, not merely to a few dedicated souls, but to the whole company of men and women who profess to love the Lord. Perhaps more than ever before, there is a present need for the Christian to be actively concerned in terms of time, money and prayer so that the underprivileged children of today may be won for Christ, growing up to become the parents of the spiritually privileged children of tomorrow. Most of all that our Lord Jesus Himself may see the travail of his soul and be satisfied.

We must now try to discover the reasons why some children of truly Christian families grow up and refuse to follow the faith of their believing parents.

Chapter Five

THOSE WHO APPEAR TO SAY NO

In spite of all that has been said about the privileges that belong to the children of Christian families, it would be unrealistic not to acknowledge that there are some boys and girls of believing parents who leave the Christian way of life in their early or late teens in spite of the fact that they appear to have been brought up in the discipline and instruction of a godly home. There is no area where reliable statistics are so few or so difficult to obtain. In theory one feels that children from a Christian home ought not to opt out, but they do. We may look upon it as a phenomenon, or the exception that proves the rule. Perhaps there is no complete answer to this complex problem. However, in seeking one, we may anticipate and even prevent the wandering of our own children. I hope to provide some consolation and encouragement to all who are at present associated with growing children, particularly those of Christian background who now seem to be rejecting Christ and His way, preferring the ways of the world.

Some people think the casualty rate is extremely high. With this I would most certainly disagree. For more than thirty years it has been my privilege, as a children's evangelist, constantly to enjoy warmhearted and generous hospitality in Christian homes up and down the country, and to be regularly associated with Christian parents and children in camps and missions. My experience is that the number of children who in growing up have rejected the faith of their parents is thankfully small. The names that I can immediately recall are less than twenty, whilst the number from Christian homes who are now integrated believers is legion. Many of these have established themselves in Christian homes of their own and are bringing up a further generation of children in the instruction and discipline of the Lord.

Andrew Murray tells of an Ebenezer Fiske, grandson of William Fiske, himself a fourth generation Christian who had emigrated to Massachusetts in 1637.[1] The son of Ebenezer was a man of inflexible religious principles. His wife was energetic and eminently pious, and would frequently set apart whole days to pray that her children might be an influence for good to the next generation. By 1857 three hundred descendants of this praying mother were members of Christian churches. For more than three hundred and thirty years the line of the holy seed had been preserved.

It may be encouraging, and I trust not out of place, to relate the personal and more recent experience of my own family. My maternal grandparents had eight children. All but one grew up to be active Christians though I believe the exception who emigrated to America never lost his love for Christ. I, myself, was one of seventeen grandchildren of whom at least fifteen have continued as active Christians. Of the next generation there are twenty-two known practising Christians. This adds up to forty-four known Christian descendants of my own grandparents while the news of the fourth generation is extremely encouraging. At the present time also, there are six or more grandchildren and great-grandchildren engaged in full-time Christian service.

For every boy and girl there must be a re-assessment of childhood beliefs and practices during the growing-up years. For many children, brought up in relaxed and integrated Christian homes, the childhood faith in Christ and their love for Him, never wavers. Outwardly there may be an apparent withdrawal due to the natural shyness and uncertainty that belong to adolescence, but inwardly the love and faith remain firm. For others there is a temporary but nevertheless extremely real, period of uncertainty and doubt – perhaps even rebellion, together with some tentative experimenting with wordly practices. Sooner or later, however, with parental understanding, patience and prayer, the majority of these teenagers will renew and ratify their childhood faith. Often they themselves think of this post-childhood commitment to God and Christ as the moment of their conversion. Conversion it certainly may be, though not the commencement of belonging, nor even the moment of regeneration. 'Unlike regeneration, conversion is a neutral word', says Cannon Stafford Wright writing on this subject. He continues, 'Conversion comes to Christians as well as to non-Christians; it is natural that it should. God has made us like this. The vital point is, to whom and to what have we been converted? The answer is, of course, to Christ and his calling. What hitherto has been a Christian form of life and belief at a parental level now becomes shot through with a dynamic experience of Father, Son and Holy Spirit, and a call to service. This teenage experience can be so exciting that it seems nothing less than regeneration. This poor vicar is told that he has not been preaching the Gospel, and there may be a transference to a "keener" church or, regrettably, the throwing up of a degree course to go immediately overseas as a missionary. This is partly, but not entirely, a caricature. More happily the new experience of Christ revives, without disrupting, the family and the church, and makes the new man or woman a concerned witness in daily life.'[2]

In this chapter, however, we are concerned with those children who tear themselves away irrevocably, as it would seem, from the Christian faith in which they have been nurtured. These, very often, were children who loved the Lord and delighted in His ways. Now they care only for this present evil world. They tend to be agnostic in their beliefs, godless and materialistic, and even immoral, in their behaviour. They often disrupt the home and break their parents' hearts. On the other hand, they may still be nice friendly people with respectable standards of life and living, but with little or no time for Christianity. The possibility of this happening is foretold in the Old Testament, and implied in the New.

In 1 Timothy 3 and Titus 1, it is clear that bishops, or elders, and deacons are ideally expected to be parents of 'believing children' which implies that some Christians may have unbelieving children.

In the Old Testament, in Ezekiel 18, after describing a righteous man, the prophet continues in verses 10–13 to declare, 'If he begets a son who is a robber, a shedder of blood . . . he shall not live. He has done all these abominable things; he shall surely die; his blood shall be upon himself.'

So the Scriptures make it abundantly clear that all the promised blessings which belong to covenant relationship, and the advantages of a Christian home, do not preclude any boy and girl from the responsibility of making an intelligent, personal ratification of faith when the compulsion occurs. The fact that concerns us is that some children say a deliberate no at this point. In doing so, they would seem to fall into a number of different classes which may be illustrated by the following examples from the Scriptures.

The Sons of Eli (1 Samuel 2:12–3:18)

The condemnation of Eli concerning his sons, who are described as 'worthless men who had no regard for the Lord', was that they blasphemed God and *he did not restrain them*. In this connection there occurs this famous statement of the Lord concerning parental responsibility, 'Those who honour me I will honour, and those who despise me shall be lightly esteemed' (1 Samuel 2:30).

It is not sufficiently realized that these solemn words were uttered by Jehovah to discipline a father who, even though he was a priest of the Lord, did not restrain the wickedness of his sons. This means that there can be no expectation of continued blessing for the children unless their Christian parents train them to distinguish clearly between right and wrong and bring them up with strict discipline in the instruction of the Lord.

It will be realized that Eli himself was not without blame.

His personal behaviour provided a possible reason for his sons' disregard for the Lord, and for their malpractices. 'Example,' said Edmund Burke, 'is the school of mankind and they will learn at no other.' This is a precept which is constantly underlined in the Scriptures. Let us not lose sight, however, of the main reason for Eli's two boys' (Hophni and Phineas) refusal to follow God. They were without parental, and especially paternal, discipline.

Many people believe that much of the present-day violence in youth stems from the fears of well-meaning parents regarding the dangers of repressing their children. Christian parents who know their Bibles should not have fallen for this kind of easy-going training for the boys and girls who have been entrusted to them by the Lord.

Ham (Genesis 9:20–10:20)

Noah was an entirely different kind of family man. Genesis 6:9 tells us that he was a righteous man, blameless in his generations, and that he walked with God. Even his regrettable post-deluge drunkenness would seem to have been the result of ignorance. Noah is mentioned more than forty times in the Old Testament, and the quality of righteousness is constantly associated with his manner of life. Yet Ham, his second son, who had been saved from the flood, together with his brothers because of his father's faith, rebelled against that faith. There is a curse upon Ham's descendants. It is generally believed that this was the direct result of his mockery of his father's drunkenness. It seems, therefore, that we must reluctantly reach the conclusion that from time to time there will be children of truly godly parents, who have experienced discipline and Christian instruction, who will deliberately choose darkness instead of light and Satan's ways instead of the ways of God.

Parents cannot be specifically blamed for this, though each will need to search his heart in the presence of the Lord. Some may even be tempted to pray that God will blot out their name rather than their child's from the book which is written. When Moses prayed like this the Lord said to him, 'Whoever has sinned against me, him will I blot out of my book.' (Exodus 32:32–33) It is clearly stated that just as children will not be put to death for the sins of their fathers so fathers may not die for the sins of their children.

Esau and Jacob (Genesis 25:19–34 and 26:34–28:22)

There is no doubt that the case of Jacob and Esau is one of the most difficult of Biblical illustrations of child–parent relationships. Here we have two brothers who are divided in their attitudes towards their parents' faith.

The statement of the Lord as recorded in Malachi 1:2–3 and Romans 9:13, 'Jacob I loved but Esau I hated' is for some unfathomable. For others it presents the complete answer to the problem we are seeking to resolve, namely election. We must not forget that side by side with God's rejection of Esau was Esau's despising of his own birthright and we must constantly remember, as we seek to reconcile the statements in the Scriptures regarding divine sovereignty and human responsibility, that God's election is based upon his foreknowledge. (See Romans 8:28–30 and Peter 1:1–2 RV)

We must also remember that Isaac and Rebekah were divided in their upbringing of the two boys. 'Isaac loved Esau, but Rebekah loved Jacob.' Parents, and especially Christian parents, must always be united and impartial in the upbringing of their children. How can they pray together for the children if there is disagreement or partiality?

It is more than likely that Isaac saw in this impetuous, warm-hearted, hairy ruffian of a son the incarnation of his own secret and unrealized fantasies. Certainly he encouraged him in his materialistic and earthy pursuits, and shared eagerly in their results. 'Isaac loved Esau because he ate of his game.' And, 'Take your quiver and your bow and hunt game for me, and prepare for me savoury food, such as I love.' It is certainly true that some modern parents have been drawn none too unwillingly into an experience of 'living it up', in order to hold on to their children during their rebellious growing-up years. Too often the final result has been disastrous for the whole family. The parents have allowed themselves to be led astray by their children at the very time the boys and girls have needed the restraint and anchorage of sustained parental principles.

While there are undoubtedly other lessons to be learnt from the history of Isaac and Rebekah and their twin sons, we must content ourselves with one final illustration. This has to do with the importance of our children's friendships. Christian children need Christian friends. Nor can the necessity for boys and girls to marry 'in the Lord' be emphasized too strongly. This is stated unmistakably by Paul: 'Do not be mismated with unbelievers. For what partnership have righteousness and iniquity? Or what fellowship has light with darkness? What accord has Christ with Belial? Or what has a believer in common with an unbeliever?' (2 Cor. 6:14–15)

Wise Christian parents, from the earliest days, will teach these principles to their sons and daughters. Otherwise they may share with their children, the sad experience of Esau who 'took to wife Judith the wife of Beeri the Hittite and Basemath the daughter of Elon the Hittite; and they made life bitter for Isaac and Rebekah'.

Observe the advice, given a hundred years ago, by Horace Bushnell, 'Let every Christian beware how he makes his children inmates of an irreligious family. It will do sometimes to allow the children of an irreligious family to be inmates temporarily in your own. You may do it for their advantage; and if you can enlist your (own) children in the merciful intention that you cherish, it may even be a good exercise for them. But it is a very different thing to place your children in the atmosphere of another house. Send them not where the spirit of evil reigns. Understand how plastic their nature is, how easily it receives the contagion of another spirit. You yourselves may have intercourse with ungodly persons; it may be your duty to seek for their benefit; but you may well be cautious how far you subject your children, especially in early years, to the intercourse of irreligious families.'[3]

While we may feel that this counsel of Bushnell is too old-fashioned for the jet-age in which we live, the scriptural principle for which he pleaded is the same today and deserves our careful thought as we consider the opportunities we allow or discourage for our children's friendships with others during their growing years.

The Prodigal Son (Luke 15:11–32)

The final history to be considered is that of the boy who ran away from home and eventually came back again. Look at the facts of his return and of the welcome he received. There have always been prodigal sons and daughters too. When the boy in the parable came to his senses and returned home, the father was waiting and watching. The robe and the ring, the shoes and the feast were all ready. 'For this my son was dead,' the father said. 'He is alive again; he was lost and is found.' It is an earthly story with a heavenly meaning. But also an earthly story with an earthly lesson as well, for it speaks of the attitude of parents to prodigals who return at last to the fold.

Forgiveness, of course is costly. 'Divine forgiveness is costly,' writes William Barclay, and he uses the following illustration of the cost of human forgiveness to demonstrate the principle. 'A son or daughter may go wrong; a father or mother may forgive; but that forgiveness has brought tears; it has brought whiteness to the hair; lines to the face; a cutting anguish, and then a long dull ache to the heart. It did not cost nothing. There was the price of the broken heart to pay.'[4] Those who are familiar with the Scottish stories of Ian Maclaren[5] will recall the bitter experience of the widower Lachlan Campbell when his daughter Flora left him all alone in his Drumtochty cottage and went away to sample the sights and sounds of London. After a time, however, and with encouragement of his godly minister and the sympathy of his fellow elders at the kirk, Lachlan was able to forgive. A letter was written to Flora. Then Lachlan himself cleaned and trimmed a lamp that was kept for show and had never been used. 'For it is in the dark that Flora will be coming, and she must know that her father is waiting for her.' Then he selected from his books Edward's 'Sinners in the hands of an angry God' and 'Coles on the Divine Sovereignty' and on them he laid the large family Bible out of which he had blotted Flora's name. 'This was the stand on which he set the lamp in the window, and every night till Flora returned its light shone down the steep path that ascended to her home, like the Divine Love from the open door of our Father's house.'

Finally, I quote Stafford Wright again, 'I am certain,' he says, 'that if our child does fall away we must as far as in us lies, keep our hearts open, the inner world in which we both have had a share.'[6] The idea of a lamp in the window is not mere sentimentality, for the wanderer often returns to the home and love that once he knew, even though both he and his parents have changed.

This means that we must never give up hope.

I want now to consider some of the hindrances to the spiritual development of children perpetuated by their parents ignorantly, thoughtlessly, selfishly or wilfully. It is a temptation to think of these in the context of other people's lives rather than our own. Yet each of us is far from perfect and, however bitter the experience, we should examine our own practices as Christian parents. Indeed many of the examples now given are regrettably gathered from my own mistakes and shortcomings as a father of four, two boys and two girls.

Hypocrisy

Piety and practice in church must be followed by consistent, practical Christ-like behaviour in the home. In *Pilgrim's*

Progress John Bunyan describes Talkative as a man who was a saint abroad and a devil at home. Too often a child reacts towards Christianity as such but towards the parents' interpretation of it.

To quote Bushnell again, 'Why is it that many persons remarkable for their piety have yet been so unfortunate in their children? Because they are yet very disagreeable persons, and that too, by reason of some very marked defect in their religious character . . . Sometimes they appear well to the world one remove distant from them, they shine well in their written biography, but one living in their family will know what others do not, and if their children turn out badly, will never be at a loss for a reason.' [7]

William Temple includes not only Christian leaders but others who have demanding responsibilities in public life – among those who show up badly with their families. He writes more sympathetically than Bushnell, 'Always there remains a self-centred area of life, and sometimes by a natural process of compensation those who are most selfless in the search for truth and beauty, or in public service, are most selfish, fretful and querulous at home.' [8]

Anxiety

When children try to interpret the anxiety shown by parents for their spiritual state or behaviour, they often feel that they are not being trusted. We must try to prevent this by believing the very best of them throughout their growing years. I have already spoken of the unhappiness that can be caused to children by workers showing undue anxiety about them. This can be a root cause of resistance and eventual rebellion.

Parental Rudeness

C. S. Lewis in *The Four Loves* has this to say about the bad manners of parents towards their children. 'We hear a great deal about the rudeness of the rising generation. I am an oldster myself and might be expected to take the oldsters' side, but in fact I have been far more impressed by the bad manners of parents to children than by those of children to parents. Who has not been the embarrassed guest at family meals where the father or mother treated their grown-up offspring with an incivility which, offered to any other young people, would simply have terminated the acquaintance? Dogmatic assertions on matters which the children understand and their elders don't, ruthless interruptions, flat contradictions, ridicule of things the young take seriously — sometimes of their religion — insulting references to their friends, all provide an easy answer to the question "Why are they always out? Why do they like every house better than their home?" Who does not prefer civility to barbarism?' [9]

It is a devastating fact that this is an attitude often adopted by Christian parents. Fathers especially project their Christian dogmatics into their family as well as into their social, business and professional lives. They themselves must be right, with the consequence that everyone who differs from them, particularly their own children, must be wrong and they feel a responsibility to tell them so. There is no surer way of spoiling good parent–child relationships, especially during the children's growing-up years.

Bushnell says: 'Alas! there are too many Christian families that are only little popedoms. The rule itself is tyranny-infallibility assumed then maintained by the holy inquisition of terror and penal chastisement. God will not smile on such a kind of discipline.' [10]

Lack of Discipline and Authority

This is the other side of the coin already considered in the context of Eli's failure to restrain the wickedness of his sons. One needs almost the wisdom of Solomon in seeking to be both firm and kind and, at the same time, absolutely fair in dealing with the children. The well-being of all the other

6

members of the family must also be borne in mind.

The Scriptures constantly warn of the foolishness of sparing the rod both literally and metaphorically, and equally of insensitively provoking our children to anger. Solomon's own precept is to be found in Proverbs 22:6; 'Train up a child in the way he should go, and when he is old he will not depart from it.'

Pettiness and Over-Correction

Our Lord spoke about this when he talked about straining at gnats and swallowing camels. Traditional puritanical prejudices often fail to distinguish between the important, clear-cut blacks and whites of wrong and right, and the unending greys which have to do with matters of dress and appearance, food and drink, spare-time activities, the pattern of Sunday observance and so on. The measure of approval or disapproval is too often based upon the criterion of what will people think, or say instead of the Ten Commandments. Children know this. It is an area which bristles with child-training problems.

Over Indulgence

Wealthy families undoubtedly are at a disadvantage here. Expensive schools, material possessions and costly holidays can very easily detract from the singleness of purpose in successful Christian living. The choice of school can be particularly significant. If this caters solely for the children of the rich the child will undoubtedly be influenced by other children there. Invitations to other children's homes may foster a desire for extravagant living. Seeds are likely to be sown which will eventually develop into a rejection of the possibly old-fashioned, unsophisticated furnishings, manners, dress, and spare-time activities in a Christian home where material possessions and secular pursuits are considered to be out of place. These dangers can usually be overcome by a sympathetic awareness and a realistic facing of the situation by parents and children together.

Immaturity

It is so easy for Christianity to be spineless and puerile. The inane laughter, and low standards of humour and conversation at many Christian social gatherings are evidences of this regrettable fact. William Barclay in a recent article emphasizing the truth that 'Life is for living', quoted George Target: 'They don't smoke but neither do they breathe fresh air very deeply. They don't drink wine, but neither do they enjoy lemonade. They don't swear, but neither do they glory in any magnificent words, neither poetry nor prayer. They don't gamble, but neither do they take much chance on God.' Christian parents in the 1970s need to offer their children a faith that is exciting, robust, intelligent and set free from an unending programme of religious meetings and the constant singing of hymns. There is a whole God-given world of music, art, drama, literature, adventure and exploration, botany, zoology and handicraft of various kinds. Woe betide the parents who fail to introduce their children to at least some of these exciting things, sharing with them the riches which God gives abundantly for each to enjoy.

Lack of Instruction

Parents also need to make sure that their children are being adequately and correctly instructed in both secular and spiritual realms. The Scriptures clearly show this to be the parents' responsibility possibly involving the father more than the mother.

Day schools and Sunday schools both have their place in the modern pattern of life, yet these do not excuse the parents from teaching their children in the quietness of the home.

Children who succeed at school are more often that not those who are encouraged at home to read and engage in intelligent conversation. Every day, if practicable, and certainly once or twice a week, there should be an unhurried, happy family meal, ideally with all the members present, and without any background of radio or television This is not to be an opportunity for catechizing or nagging the children or dealing with family problems. Someone once said that conversational contention at meal times was a sure recipe for ulcers.

In our own family we deliberately try to keep problem sessions away from the meal table and have found this to be extremely profitable.

It is not sufficiently realized that relaxed unhurried conversation divorced from contention can be a satisfying and beneficial art. It is an accomplishment to be acquired, cultivated and taught within the close-knit relationships of the family. Too often this is sadly neglected.

This family meal with no one monopolizing the conversation should be a time when parents and children and visitors happily relate the happenings of the day, share the experiences of books, outings and projects and, if it arises naturally, the tokens of God's love and care. No one is left out. There is no unkindly ignoring of the younger, shyer or visiting members. The father and mother together make sure of this as they skilfully and imperceptibly encourage everyone to join in and take part. This unhurried meal-time is also the best opportunity for shared family reading of the Scriptures and for prayer. These need to be relaxed and happy as well as solemn and reverent. During this time there must be no traumatic change of mood, no alteration in the tone of voice, particularly when the children are young. The time must be kept quite short and no diversion allowed. Children will benefit tremendously from sharing these activities with their parents. They foster a reciprocal respect which cannot help but influence the permanence of the children's spiritual faith.

No Time for the Children

A father who was working hard to save his marriage said to me recently, 'If only I could give as much time to my marriage as I give to my business, all would be well.'

A growing-up girl from a Christian home said bitterly, 'My father does nothing but go to meetings.'

Many Christian parents are far too busy to give adequate time to their children. They engage in money-making activities in an endeavour to 'keep up with the Joneses'. Not merely the Joneses in the world but also those in the local church. Even Christian activities can be overdone and unintentionally prevent children enjoying more of their parents' time and interest.

There is a failure in the assessment of priorities here. At least two young wives have told me of the near breakdown in the early days of their marriages simply because they and their husbands had taken on more than their fair share of responsibilities in the church. This left no time to relax with each other and with their children at home. Keith Miller devotes two chapters of *Habitation of Dragons*[11] to this important subject, and tells how he straightened out his own priorities by writing into his new calendar his wedding anniversary, the family birthdays and times for family outings and holidays, before any speaking or other outside engagements. 'I remember,' he writes, 'the first time an invitation to participate in a big meeting came on one of the children's birthdays. I was very interested in the meeting but said, "No". The man who was a friend, must have sensed my hesitation, because he asked, "Why can't you come? This is an important convention and your witness might reach a lot of people." I was a little embarrassed to say that it was my little girl's birthday but I went on to tell him, "You can get half a dozen speakers but I'm the only daddy she's got". He was quiet on the other end of the line for a few seconds and I thought he had rejected me as a fool. Then he said quietly, "I wish I could do that", and I knew that I had begun in the right direction.'

The Bible clearly shows that family men and women have a first responsibility to each other and to their children, and it is encouraging to discover that more and more churches are planning Sunday programmes with the afternoon entirely free so that parents and children together can spend this part of the 'different day' in unhurried family activity. This also is a requisite for spiritual family stability.

Lack of Security

Children with friends from broken homes cannot help dreading the possibility of their own home breaking up. They can know even greater insecurity if they are living in a Christian home, where, for the sake of appearances, the parents are staying together yet failing to resolve the constant friction and lack of harmony. A girl of eleven who came from a Christian home where there had been a prolonged period of parental quarrelling, burst into tears in my presence and said, 'I know what is going to happen; Mum and Dad are going to leave each other.' Fortunately the situation was shortlived, and I believe the child's insecurity was resolved. But it shows the kind of situation which can so easily arise and hinder the faith of a child in God.

It was reported in the *Daily Telegraph* on October 15th, 1973 that 'Quarrelling parents are driving many children and teenagers to the point of suicide according to the Samaritans.' The report went on to say that the Samaritans are getting more and more calls from desperate children who say they cannot stand rows at home any longer. 'Children get upset when parents quarrel,' the Samaritans' secretary is quoted as saying, 'particularly the very young. We have had calls from children of nine, ten, eleven and twelve. The youngest was a child of eight.'

A Wrong Motive

Of course we want the best for our children – there can be nothing wrong in that. This responsibility has been laid upon us by God himself who has entrusted the children to us. In wanting the best for them, it is essential that we want God's best, not our own. Father and mother together should pray both morning and evening for each child by name. Their prayer should embrace every single member of their family, seeking God's best for each.

The concern of the mothers of Solomon and of James and John for their sons is significant here.

Many years ago, when our own children were growing up, I bought and read *Finney on Revivals of Religion*. I have never forgotten his strong plea for proper motives in praying, both on the part of the church for the unsaved, and on the part of parents for their children. The true motive must always be the glory of God. I quote, 'The temptation to selfish motives is so strong that there is reason to fear a great many parental prayers never rise above the yearnings of parental tenderness. And this is the reason why so many pious praying parents have ungodly children.' [12] And again, 'The supreme motive must be to honour and glorify God ... thus parents may be agreed in prayer for the conversion of their children, and may have the same feelings and the same motives, and yet if they have no higher motives than because they are *their children* their prayers will not be granted. They agreed in the reason but it is not the right reason.' [13] At the same time it must not be forgotten that, as parents, we do have this God-given responsibility towards our own children. Our special and prayerful concern for them particularly, is by no means misplaced. But our motive must be to honour and glorify God. This is the important, safeguarding principle.

Boasting Parents

Parents tend to boast about their own children. All our geese are swans and we do not hesitate to say so. I have known Christian families where even the children themselves have been deceived and have been encouraged by their parents' fine talking to think of themselves as superior beings. As they grow older, the parents' boastings become a constant embarrassment, a hindrance to their walking humbly with the Lord.

I cannot help wondering about the wisdom of sending detailed material in the family news letters which are circulated widely at Christmas time. A general reference to the health and progress of the children is fair enough, but details about John's and Mary's exploits, their prowess in the realms of games, their exams and spare time activities cannot help but read like glorification for its own sake. It is a false projection of the child's natural importance. It is liable to be strongly disliked by healthy minded sons and daughters as they grow older and provides one more stumbling block.

In no other sphere of our Christian parental responsibilities do we need more urgently the sympathetic encouragement provided by our Lord; 'My grace is sufficient for you, for my power is made perfect in weakness.' (2 Corinthians 12:9)

Chapter Six

SIN AND REPENTANCE

As I look back over more than forty years of working with children, and nearly thirty years as a children's evangelist, I am sure that the subjects which have given me an increasing concern since earliest days, both in content and presentation, have been those of sin and repentance. For many years I held rigidly to the traditional patterns. But I have come to realize that many of these are adult in concept and are generally unsuitable for children and incomprehensible to them. At the same time I have become increasingly aware of the importance of a proper understanding on the part of teachers and parents of the true Bible meanings of sin, guilt, and condemnation on the one hand, and repentance on the other, as they are applied to children. It is far from easy for any of us to break away from what has been said for so many years in handbooks and children's booklets, and it is only after considerable thought and study that I have arrived at the following conclusions. I believe these to be thoroughly scriptural in content, sensible and relevant in their application to boys and girls.

Sin

The word, *sin*, may no longer be used without careful definition. It may have a very real meaning for each of us. It is more than likely that it has a particular sound, and that we have a special, significant, not to say sinister, way of saying, 'SIN'. However, for older as well as younger folk, the actual

English word is ambiguous and at times incomprehensible. For most teenagers and many children it is a word used to describe wrong and perverted adulterous relationships between the sexes, and it is limited to this usage. 'Living in sin' is the old-fashioned phrase which has become a modern designation for men and women co-habiting outside wedlock.

For some children also it has more recently become a synonym for pollution. A boy aged ten gave me a competition paper decorated in colour with factory chimneys belching out smoke. Underneath he had written the single word SIN.

Clearly the word no longer has its original biblical meaning, and we must look for a different word. The words evil or bad are unsuitable because each has ambiguous connotations. The word wrong however is straightforward enough, and is clearly understood as being the opposite to right. So these are the most suitable words for using with children – WRONG – WRONGDOER – WRONGDOING

Notice how adequately the word wrongdoing translates six of the words which are used in the New Testament to describe the activities of the fallen state of mankind. These are usually translated in the Authorized Version as follows:

1. Sin (Gr. *hamartia*), with the meaning of missing the mark or falling below a recognized standard. Romans 6:23

2. Transgression (Gr. *parabasis*), with the meaning of stepping over a line – a deviation. Hebrews 2:2.

3. Trespass (Gr. *paraptoma*), with the meaning of slipping up – a blunder. Ephesians 2:1

4. Lawlessness (Gr. *anomia*). It means what it says. 'Sin is lawlessness'. 1 John 3:4

5. A Debt (Gr. *opheile*). Again it means what it says. It is a sin of omission. 'Forgive us our debts, as we forgive our debtors.' Matthew 6:12

6. Unrighteousness (Gr. *adikia*). It also has the meaning of injustice and iniquity. Romans 1:18

All these are the outworkings of what we call original sin or inborn sinfulness. They are seen in the life of a child, and are positive proof that the nature of the child is depraved and that there is need for forgiveness and renewal. Wrongdoing would certainly seem to be as good a word as any to describe each of these activities, though we are likely to continue to use the word sin when appropriate. Indeed since I am not writing for children, I shall use the word in the remainder of this chapter.

Guilt

It is also true to say that the child is guilty. But we must make sure that we understand what we mean by the use of this word. Guilt is not simply a subjective feeling of shame which an individual may have after having done something wrong. Neither is it the business of the teacher or preacher to stir up such a feeling in the mind of a child. Guilt, in the true biblical sense, is an objective description of an individual's status before God when measured by the law. It is a state of condemnation or punishment – 'All the world guilty before God', (Romans 3:19 KJ). Compare the Revised Standard Version of the Bible, 'Held accountable to God', and the New English Bible, 'Exposed to the judgment of God'. It is sometimes called blameworthiness.

Although these things which have to do with original sin and guilt are essential for our knowledge of the state of a child apart from Christ, it does not mean that we should explain them in detail to children any more than a doctor shares the intricacies of a diagnosis with his patient. While it is essential for the sinful child and the sick patient to be aware of their condition, the important thing for both is the proper remedy.

Anyone who works with people needs to have the most profound knowledge of his subject. Yet every good teacher, doctor, lawyer or lecturer knows that any attempt to impart too much too soon is bound to produce confusion and unhappiness. Compare our Lord's words to his disciples, 'I have many things to say to you, but you cannot bear them now.' (John 16:12). Notice how William Barclay translates Mark 4:33, 'He kept speaking the word to them, suiting his instruction to their ability to hear it.'

Before we can begin to list the kind of things that we shall expect to teach the children about their sinful state and sinful conduct, it is imperative that we possess an informed opinion of the behaviour patterns that belong to different groups of adults and children. These may be classified as follows:

1. Deliberate rejection of God and disobedience to His Will.

2. The outworkings of original sin apart from the consent of the will.

3. The infection of original sin which remains in those who are regenerated.

4. Children's naughtiness.

In the past there has been an over-emphasis placed on Paul's important declaration, recorded in Romans 3:23 that, 'There is no distinction; since all have sinned and fall short of the glory of God.' This basic scriptural concept has been used in isolation and with no proper distinction in thought or presentation between responsible adults and irresponsible children. Such an umbrella-type application of a single statement can be dangerously misleading, as I hope to show in the following development of the behaviour pattern analysis.

1. *Deliberate Rejection of God and Disobedience to His Will*

The sin which has always brought the individual under the condemnation of Jehovah is a refusal to acknowledge and honour God in the light of the revelation He has so graciously given of himself to mankind. This is clearly declared in Romans 1:18–32. It finds its expression in the individual who having been presented with the Gospel deliberately rejects Christ. See John 3:16–21 and 16:9.

John 3 verse 19 sums it up for us, 'And this is the judgment, that the light has come into the world, and men loved darkness rather than light, because their deeds were evil.'

It is most important to realize that this condemnation which belongs to wilful rebellion cannot possibly apply to children before they have reached the age of intelligent discretion and accountability.

2. *The Outworking of Original Sin Apart from the Consent of the Will*

The first essential here is to appreciate that in God's sight the sin of the individual 'may be considered abstractedly from the person in whom it resides.' See Romans 5:13 which says that sin is not counted where there is no law.

All of us whatever our denominational persuasions, may be thankful for the careful wording of the Anglican Article concerning what is called, 'Original or Birth Sin'. It says this, 'In every person born into the world it deserveth God's wrath and condemnation.' [1]

It is important to notice the word *'it'* by which the statement distinguishes between the sinner and his sin. Notice too, the accuracy of the word *'deserveth'* which emphasizes what sin is *entitled* to receive, though it does not say that every case of inborn sinfulness will actually receive the Divine judgment. This also is scripturally accurate.

'My sins deserve eternal death, but Jesus died for me.' is an old saying remembered from my own childhood. In Chapter One I have already quoted George Goodman's saying: 'In the resurrection all irresponsible persons, infants and others, will have no charge against them, and can therefore be the objects of that free grace that comes through the reconciliation made at Calvary.' [2]

It is also helpful to compare again what Griffith Thomas has to say in this connection as he comments on the Article. 'Children are born with an evil nature in a state of what is called depravity, and when reason dawns they know something of right and wrong, though they have only a partial responsibility, but in course of time they become fully responsible for the sin of their own will.' [3] He continues:

'While everyone is born into the world with the evil principle within derived and inherited, it is only as the individual asserts himself and does what is wrong that he is personally subject to the Divine condemnation. In whomsoever it is found even as a latent potentiality, it must in itself be an object of God's displeasure, but it does not follow that the person must be so, still less that the sentence on sin will in such a case be inflicted. The tendency which, if the infant lives, will assuredly give birth to actual sin, cannot in God's sight be a thing indifferent; but as it is only an objective guiltiness (to which the will has not consented because the individual is incapable of will) it may be covered by an objective Atonement (not yet appreciated by an act of will) so that the infant himself is not, and never has been an object of God's wrath.' [4]

The teaching here is that there is a big difference between the inevitable, unintentioned outworkings of inborn sinfulness in the behaviour pattern of a child before the age of discretion and the wilful sinfulness described above. This means that the child is unlikely, in a truly accurate sense, to be 'a guilty, lost and hell-deserving sinner', and we must beware of thinking this and not speak of it.

'If I am to become a Christian, I must own up and tell God I am a guilty sinner' is a statement taken from a widely used children's booklet. This is not true for a large majority of children and must be incomprehensible to most of them. We must speak, tenderly and sensitively to children of the seriousness of their wrongdoing. We must show how sin is, in fact, sin against God and then go on to teach the importance and the need of forgiveness. Constantly in our thinking there must be this distinction between culpable adult wilful rebellion and a child's inherent but undetermined wrong-doing. Objective guiltiness will be covered objectively from God's sight by His sovereign grace and by the reconciliation made at Calvary.

As Griffith Thomas says, 'Surely the truth is that all children are included in the great atoning sacrifice and belong to Jesus Christ until they deliberately refuse him.' [5]

Therefore, in our speaking and teaching, we must avoid

traditional generalizations and sweeping statements concerning guilt and condemnation, and be positive in our presentation of the Saviourhood of Christ and His offer of forgiveness. In addition, our Lord's promise of help by the Holy Spirit, will form a constant, complementary part of our teaching, so that the child may positively and joyfully discover how to do the things that are good and right and true.

As we study with the children the actual Bible passages which deal with sin and its consequences, we must be careful always to distinguish between the intelligently mature adult and the latent child.

3. The infection of Original Sin which remains in those who are regenerated

This is the third of my four divisions of the outworkings of original sin. Sadly because of its reality we must agree with the following quotation from Article IX of the book of Common Prayer, 'This infection of nature doth remain, yea, in them that are regenerated.' This needs to be considered as it will help us to adopt a proper, scriptural attitude towards the children and their behaviour.

All too easily as Christian parents and teachers, although we are grieved by the evidences of original sin in the lives of our children, we conveniently forget the inconsistencies that belong to our own. Side by side with the recollection of our children's disobedience and quarrelsomeness we need to remember our own impatience, bad temper and other shortcomings.

Horace Bushnell puts it like this, '. . . have you nothing to blame in yourselves – no lack of faithfulness – no mistakes of duty which with a better and more cultivated piety you would have been able to avoid?' And again, 'A child acts out his present feelings of the moment without qualification or disguise; and how many times would all you appear if you were to do the same?' [6]

The important thing here is that the wrong things in our

children's lives, or in our own for that matter, are not necessarily evidences of being unregenerate. It may well be for them as for us that 'the infection of nature that doth remain, yea, in them that are regenerated.'

Our children, who may not yet have consciously believed, should be taught to confess their sins to Christ and so experience the forgiveness of God. A forgiveness based wholly on the atoning and finished work of Calvary. There is a valuable opportunity here for parents and children to confess their wrongdoings to God audibly together.

Naughtiness

Here we may have no scriptural authority but we must recognize the fine distinction that can exist in the wrongdoing of children. On the one hand there are disobedience, stealing, untruthfulness and the like and on the other the outworkings of childhood exuberance and tiredness, giving rise to high spirits, mischievousness, fretfulness and moodiness. Even apparent untruthfulness can be due to the happy, though sometimes embarrassing, gift of a vivid imagination, nor is childhood stealing or disobedience always vicious. Some of the behaviour patterns that appal us in children belong to what has been called the 'Juvenile Jungle', and often would seem to be necessary if the child is to survive! As children's workers we must remember that what we may well call the revolting manners and behaviour of less intelligent children from rough environments do not mean that these boys and girls are more wicked than their apparently nicely behaved brothers and sisters from a better neighbourhood. Patience, wisdom, sympathy, discernment and unending love are needed here. We must be careful not to be vindictive nor to use the threat of eternal judgment and condemnation as a means of retaliation or restraint.

With our teaching to the children about their sinful state and their sinful behaviour still in mind, there are three further safeguards which need to be remembered.

1. We must not have an adult approach. This is an underlining of what has already been said. I have become more and more convinced that the mistakes that are constantly made in the spiritual teaching of children occur because we ignore the difference of approach that is necessary between an adult and a child. The genius of our Lord's teaching was his discerning approach to a wide variety of people. He said quite different things to Zacchaeus, Nicodemus, the Samaritan woman and the rich young ruler. In contrast our own teaching to children often has an uninspiring sameness about it simply because it is a presentation of watered down adult notions with little appreciation that much of what is said is unintelligible and irrelevant to a child.

The idea that every bit of the Bible is to be included in the syllabus for children is soon exploded when we bear in mind the inexpedience of including, for example, an explanation of the story of Tamar, or the sins of Sodom and Gomorrah. Children will also need to grow up before they can properly comprehend the true biblical meanings of guilt and condemnation, of the Blood of Christ and of the Holiness of God, to give but a few examples. We must never imagine that a child, or a grown up person for that matter, cannot become a real Christian until these are understood. This does not mean that these great Bible themes will never be mentioned. Many children are remarkably perceptive as they are led and taught by the Holy Spirit. Let us, however, always remember the Bible way as we read in Isaiah 28:10. It is precept upon precept upon precept, line upon line, here a little, there a little.

2. We must not be flippant. Sin must never be spoken of in a light-hearted manner. Sometimes, regrettably, children's speakers are guilty of playing to an adult gallery. A story is told of a boy or girl which involves a description of laziness, disobedience or bad temper and is told in such a way that it often deliberately produces laughter from part of the audience. Usually it is the adults who laugh. The children are

7

sensitive about their own and their fellows' wrongdoing. But sin is never funny. It is the abominable thing which God hates (Jeremiah 44:4). There should always be a sober and sensitive presentation of this truth.

Incidentally, it is unwise ever to accept an adult's assessment of the success of a children's talk. The parents may have been amused and entertained whilst the children have received little or nothing.

3. We must not sermonize all the time. In the January/ March 1972 issue of the Scripture Union magazine *Outreach*, a mother wrote, ' "I'm sick of the crucifixion", complained Junior one evening at bedtime. He glanced at me cautiously wondering if I might be horrified at the remark. I wasn't. In the early part of the year it had been stretched over three weeks of lessons at Sunday School. At Easter the story was repeated, and here we were again covering the same ground in the daily readings.'

The story of this wonderful happening at Calvary had become tarnished by too constant repetition. This can be devastatingly true of all great Bible themes and of the constant reiteration to 'Let Jesus come in'. We must be careful also to give teaching on sin its proper place and not to be always speaking of it.

I come now to what I believe a child should be taught both progressively and objectively about sin and its consequence. The more I think about this the more I realize the inadequacy of one chapter in a book. It really requires a book on its own. All I can do is to set down what I believe should be the basic ingredients.

The Fact of Wrongdoing

This is likely to be the most relevant part of our teaching to children about sin. It is a problem even to the youngest child who readily admits, 'I try so hard to be good, and I'm not.'

It is possible here, with the age of the children always in mind, to teach about the nature of evil and to show that 'I am not a sinner because I sin, but I sin because I am a sinner.' Older children will be able to follow this simple logic; 'It is not an apple tree because it bears apples; but it bears apples because it has the root and nature of an apple tree.' The seriousness of wrongdoing must always be solemnly taught, underlining that all sin is sin against God. It can be shown, for example, that the turning point for the Prodigal Son was the moment when he realized that he had run away not only from his father's will but from God's will – 'I have sinned *against heaven* and before you.'

The emphasis in our teaching should be on the willingness of the Lord Jesus to forgive with regard to the past, and to enable with regard to the present. Such an emphasis must be made in the context of Christ's death and resurrection.

When teaching about the new life care must be taken not to give the impression that the old is entirely taken away. Often an impression is left with the boys and girls by eager yet mistaken speakers that once you have said 'Yes' to Jesus you will live happily ever afterwards. The child soon finds that this simply does not happen, and feels that he has been deceived. Children constantly talk and write to me about this. They must be shown that positive Christian living is far from easy and that there is a continual conflict between the flesh and the Spirit.

At the same time is should also be taught, as in the words of a Salvation Army song, that –

Jesus is stronger than Satan and sin;
Satan to Jesus must bow;
And I have the victory without and within,
For Jesus is saving me now.

The availability of moment to moment forgiveness is an essential part of the teaching based on 1 John 1:9 'If we confess our sins, He is faithful and just and will forgive our sins and cleanse us from all unrighteousness.' This text must not be used as a 'Way' verse for first coming to the Saviour. Rather it should be used to show the children the day to day experience of claiming forgiveness and cleansing that can be theirs. We should also stress the need for godly sorrow.

The Consequences of Wrongdoing

I have come to realize that it is unwise to place a constant emphasis upon eternal judgment as a consequence of sin, with a reiteration of the first part of Romans 6:23 that the wages of sin is death. These are adult concepts which are likely to be unintelligible to any but the older children, while the strongly entrenched idea that there must always be conviction of sin is both unscriptural and untrue.

The more senior boys and girls should, from time to time, be taught something of the final experience of those who reject Christ. This, most probably, will be described as being separation from God, though the parent or teacher should be quite clear in his own mind what this means. It is also important to bear in mind that prior to the age of responsibility a child 'is not and never has been an object of God's wrath' even though by nature he is linked to the first Adam. In God's sight he is covered by the Atonement. The consequences of sin which belong to the child's own experience are those of unhappiness and conflict in the home, with a resultant grieving of parents and the spoiling of relationships. From these it may be shown that to do wrong is also grieving to God, wrongdoing separates us from God in the sense that we become out of tune with Him. Our friendship is broken.

We have wandered from the fold and though we are not yet perishing, (Matthew 18:12–14), we have 'gone astray'.

The Greatest Sin

The most important thing to teach the older children is that the greatest sin is to break the first commandment, which is to love the Lord your God with all your heart, with all your mind and with all your strength. From this there naturally follows the importance of saying, 'Yes' to the Lord Jesus, and the significance of saying, 'No', or even nothing at all.

The word used in Scripture to denote sin is unbelief. This is vividly described in Romans chapter 1. It means saying, 'No' when God says, 'Yes', saying, 'Yes' when God says, 'No'. It embraces the rejection of God, his love, his claims, his truth, and finally his Christ. These are the things that expose the individual to judgment. Although they belong to the age of discretion and responsibility they should be taught objectively to all children. The whole purpose of spiritual instruction to children is to enable them to escape from judgment by learning to say, 'Yes' to Jesus, without pressure, without undue anxiety and at a very early age.

As the child grows up our sense of love and urgency will grow too as we realize that a consistant refusal to say, 'Yes' must eventually be regarded as a deliberate rejection. Before they leave Junior school, the boys and girls who have been regularly taught the things of God can be expected to make a decision, either accepting or rejecting Christ. I must emphasize, that we must still not be tempted into separating the sheep from the goats. This would be presumption. The Lord alone knows who are His.

Nor must we persistently seek to harass a child who appears unresponsive. Prayer, faith, love and patience are the important things for a teacher to possess. Remember that the less extrovert children will probably have an experience of conscious response later on.

Right and Wrong

We also need to teach the moral importance of doing right and refusing to do wrong.

Montaigne wrote in his biography, 'Children should be taught to hate vice for its own texture, so that they will not only avoid it in action, but abominate it in their hearts.'

Careful teaching about the relevance and true meaning of the Ten Commandments has never been more necessary than it is today. Things like stealing, violence, disobedience to parents, greed, coveteousness, untruthfulness, blasphemy and particularly Godlessness must form an important part of our teaching about sin. The facts of right and wrong, as revealed in the Bible, must be taught to children in a dispassionate way. Evidence of inborn sinfulness and a demonstration of the child's need of forgiveness and of God, these facts can be presented as a challenge to do right.

It cannot be stressed too strongly that it is the work of the Holy Spirit to convince of sin. 'When He comes He will convince the world of sin, of righteousness, and of judgment' (John 16:8). We may pray for and hope for this conviction, but we must remember that it is not the responsibility of the parent or teacher to create it.

There must be no vindictiveness in our teaching. We must avoid painting a word picture of a stern, relentless, faultfinding God with a big stick who needs to be persuaded by the Lord Jesus to be forgiving. It is God who loves the world so much that he sent his Son; it is God who laid our sins on Jesus; it is God who raised him from the dead; it is God who 'has all men penned together in the prison of disobedience, that he may have mercy upon them all' (Romans 11:32; J. B. Phillips).

William Barclay has a timely warning of the distorted version of the Gospel that has been presented to men and women so that there is a division in their minds between God and Jesus. 'They have come to look on God,' he says, 'as a person to be feared and Jesus as a person to be loved. They have felt at home with Jesus, but strange and uncomfortable and scared of God. They have looked on Jesus as their defence and rescuer from the wrath of God. So deeply is this ingrained into the minds of some people in their younger days that they never wholly grow out of it. They feel that Jesus is indeed their friend, but they are haunted rather than helped by the very thought of God.'[7] So let us beware! We ought not to be surprised to find that it is extremely rare for any child to have a deep sense of sin. Much more likely are a sense of need because of loneliness or an inability to get on with people, or unhappiness in the home, or a deeply fixed anti-social attitude shown by the child. We are all familiar with the comments that give expression to these: 'Everyone is horrid to me.' 'No one wants to be my friend.' 'Mum and Dad are always quarrelling.' 'Mum is always nagging me.' 'I keep losing my temper.' 'I am always quarrelling with my brother or sister.'

Children whose confidence I have gained often talk quite spontaneously about such unhappinesses which are much more common that is often realized. Invariably it is the sense of need that is uppermost, rarely a sense of sin. Although the ultimate solution is the friendship and help of Jesus, possible immediate help at a human level must not be neglected. The important thing to remember is that in our declaration of the love and power of Jesus we must avoid the mistake of insisting upon a sense of sin before allowing any individual to make a response to the Saviour.

A. Paget-Wilkes, in his book *Dynamic of Service*, compares the experience of an individual's sense of need with his sense of sin. 'I have been perfectly astonished,' he says, 'at how many souls have come to Christ, their subsequent life proving that their conversion is real and genuine, without any sense of sin at all.'[8] We find that this also was true for most of the individuals we meet in the New Testament — Nicodemus, the Samaritan woman, Zacchaeus. Even the Philippian gaoler who cried, 'What must I do to be saved?' was undoubtedly thinking, at that moment, much more about his culpable involvement with the opened prison doors than with his sins. But notice how his sense of need was used by Paul and Silas as a means to lead him to the Saviour. In this of course, they followed the example of Jesus. We must do the same. This has certainly been my own experience in seeing many children responding to the Lord over the years. There has been a real sense of need, but very rarely a sense of sin.

I recall being with a group of intelligent teenagers, the majority of whom were Christians. As a basis of our Bible study, we were using *Pilgrim's Progress* and arising out of this the group was asked how many had a 'burden of sin' when they accepted Christ as Saviour. Not one confessed to this. They spoke of a sense of need at this time. Any sense of sinfulness came later.

The teaching of the cross must be closely linked to our teaching of the forgiveness of sin. We can use the Old Testament pictures such as the Ark, the Blood Sprinkled Door, the Brazen Serpent, Jacob's Ladder and the offering of Isaac to illustrate the New Testament facts of the atonement, for the subject defies illustration other than that taken from the Bible. We must refuse to cheapen this tremendous happening by using any feeble man-made anecdote even though we may find the subject difficult to teach and explain.

The stark fact that He bore our sins in His own body on the cross, with a simple reverent account of the event is all that is needed. We must avoid all sadistic details and over-dramatization.

Someone has said that there is more true teaching about the atoning work of Christ in Mrs Alexander's beautiful children's hymn than in any other writing of comparable length:

He died that we might be forgiven;
He died to make us good;
That we might go at last to heaven,
Saved by his precious blood.

I often invite the children to recite those words quietly with me in a meeting. They usually know them by heart. It is an effective way of emphasizing this important truth.

Following the example of the apostles in the Acts, we should rarely, if ever, teach the Crucifixion without the Resurrection. He is the *living* Lord Jesus who died. He is the real though invisible friend who is near at hand to enable and to bless.

The difficult and complementary Bible teaching concerning the high priestly work of the risen and ascended Christ at the right hand of God should also find its place in our teaching of the older children. Do let us realize however that the Victorian concept of a Heaven and a friend for little children 'above the bright blue sky' is both misleading and inaccurate (not to say unacceptable) to intelligent space-age children. I loved this hymn when I was a child and I know what I mean when I sing it nostalgically over to myself. So I am as sad as anyone that it has to be dismissed from the children's repertoire.

Repentance

It is not surprising to find that repentance in its true scriptural meaning has little or no place in the experience of a child. Repentance, in the biblical meaning of the word, is much more than sorrow, regret or remorse. Literally, repentance is a change of mind and heart. It carries the meaning of second thoughts in the active response to God in turning from sin. Repentance is continuous and progressive. It is dependant upon a developing knowledge of the meaning of sin and the person and character of God.

Martin Luther said, 'I never knew repentance until I learned it from the wounds of Jesus.' And I have discovered that for very many Christians their experience of true biblical repentance has been a post-conversion experience. Undoubtedly this is because it is not possible to have repentance any more than faith, in a vacuum. Acts 20:21 tells us that it is 'repentance towards God.' Therefore it requires some knowledge of the character and holiness of God which an individual, and certainly a child, is not likely to have in the beginning.

The use in the New Testament of the Greek word *metanoia* for repentance is surprising. It occurs only 24 times as a noun and 34 times as a verb. The word does not occur at all in John's Gospel and only once in the Epistle to the

Romans. It is used mostly to the Pharisees, sometimes to the Jews, never directly to an individual. There is no recorded call to repent to Zacchaeus, to the woman of Samaria, to Mary Magdalene, to Cornelius, or to the Philippian gaoler. There is an implied need for repentance to the rich young ruler, but to no other individual who was counselled by our Lord or his apostles. This does not mean that repentance is unimportant. But it is not essential, at least consciously, for conversion. Similarly we cannot prevent an individual from coming to Christ because he has no proper conviction of sin.

'After all,' says Bishop Ryle in *Knots Untied*, 'will any one tell us that an intelligent profession of repentance and faith is absolutely necessary to salvation?' [9]

Experience shows that this is especially true of children. With a child's limited knowledge and comprehension of the character and holiness of God, it cannot be otherwise.

We must also remember that for the children of Christian homes, whose earliest thoughts have been directed positively and lovingly towards the Saviour, there will be no place for second thoughts or the change of direction widely accepted as conversion repentance. There are many children who have loved the Saviour for as long as they can remember and have said, 'Yes' to Him from the beginning of their conscious existence. With less fortunate children in mind, we can certainly use the thought of repentance in the presentation of our message, whilst avoiding the use of this difficult theological word. There are many children whose great need is to be turned from darkness to light and from the power of Satan to God. They may not be able to comprehend this, or even realize what has happened until long after it has taken place. We must not hesitate, therefore, to teach the importance of being sorry for immediate wrongdoing and a willingness to turn from self-centred bad behaviour when coming to Jesus. For godly sorrow is certainly an ingredient of repentance. But we must remember that even this may not be evident when a child says, 'Yes' to Jesus.

It may be argued that any experience of turning to Christ is an implied act of repentance, even though the individual is unaware of its being so. I agree. I think this is the answer to those who insist on repentance being always present at conversion.

We might use the illustration of a traveller in a storm at night. Seeking refuge in a lighted haven he turns from the road along which he has been journeying, unaware of the fact that a little way on is a precipice. He leaves the road with a tinge of regret that he started the journey at all. He certainly feels sorry for himself unhappily caught in the storm and darkness. He has no knowledge of the danger to which he had been exposed, yet this did not hinder or prevent his 'salvation'.

In teaching the older children of the character and holiness of God and of the biblical meaning of sin, we must not be surprised to discover their growing consciousness of the reality of sin. There will also be a deeper love for the Lord and a more sensitive appreciation of all that Jesus came to say and to do. These are the evidences of true repentance even though we may not insist on them as being essential for salvation in either our preaching or personal work.

Remember then that because of its expanded meaning and ambiguous usage the word repentance is not really suitable for inclusion in our general teaching. It should be used only to well-informed adults and even then not without careful definition.

'Repentence plus Faith equals Conversion', is a cosy and traditional definition which is unsuitable for children. True repentance is often a post conversion occurrence, while faith, by its very nature, is synonymous with response. It may be a faith that is as small as a mustard seed and the individual who exercises it may not even realize that it is faith or understand its spiritual significance. Nevertheless 'without faith it is impossible to please God.' This is so important that we must consider its meaning for the child in another chapter.

Chapter Seven

THE RESPONSE OF THE CHILD

There is no doubt that the ideal conscious response of a child to Christ will be spontaneous and uncomplicated. It should not be spoilt by the demands of unwise adults for some traditional or specific procedure. Nor should we insist on there being a conviction of sin, acts of repentance or even a stereotyped expression of faith. 'Last night I felt I wanted to throw my arms around Jesus.' This was the spontaneous response described in a letter by a ten-year old girl during a children's mission.

The same kind of response is expressed in these verses from Miss E. R. Swain, one-time headmistress of Clarendon School.

The Saviour found me in his boundless grace
Before I even knew that I was lost.
My tiny footsteps scarcely had begun
To tread the path of danger ere I saw
The Shepherd close beside me. 'Twas enough.
No sense of danger made me seek His arms,
I did but catch a glimpse of His dear face,
Then gladly let Him lift me to his breast,
And only after that when I was safe,
And felt his arms encircling me with love,
Did he himself point out the road below.
I saw His love before I saw my need;
I knew my safety long before I knew
The awful death from which He rescued me;
And though I cannot tell when this took place,

Or when I first was clasped in His embrace,
I only know He found me – I am His.

It is encouraging that many children with happy relaxed
Christian backgrounds respond just like this. Their experience
is similar to that of young Campbell Morgan described in
Chapter One. 'When the necessity came for my personal
choosing,' he declares, 'so did I recognize the claims of His
love, that without revulsion, and hardly knowing when, I
yielded to Him my allegiance and my love.' Dr Morgan's
childhood experience underlines the all-important truth that
when a child from a Christian family makes a conscious
committal to Christ it is really the appropriation of something
which has already taken place. It is the culmination of a
response, progressive from the earliest years to the love of
God. For many such children there is no crisis experience at
all; simply a time when they happily enter into the conscious
assurance of belonging. The unfolding flower is now wide
open to the sun. There is rarely an awareness of sinfulness
and repentance until much later.

This can also be true of many children from non-Christian
backgrounds who have been prayerfully taught and cared for
in the fellowship of our churches and Sunday schools. Their
first experience of faith and response is wholly occupied with
the person of Christ and their desire to belong to Him.
Counselling or any form of cross-questioning is superfluous.
Once the child has experienced the call of Christ and has
understood how to say, 'Yes,' the response is made. Ideally it
will be a private transaction between the child and the Lord
without any immediate adult interference or assistance. Over
the years I have found this to be the experience of numerous
children attending my own missions.

'I became a Christian last night in bed,' wrote a ten-year-
old girl during a village mission.

'I asked Jesus to come into my heart last night in my
prayers,' wrote a thirteen-year-old boy during a city mission.

Often one does not know what has happened until long
afterwards. Recently, during my third mission at a church, a

fifteen year old girl wrote to say how she and her older sister had both come to Christ during my first visit seven years previously. Two others wrote to say that they had said 'Yes', to Jesus during the previous mission two and a half years before. There had been no counselling, no cross-questioning, yet they were all growing up happily in a live church.

At another church, during a weekend return visit, a growing boy came up to me and said,'I am a Christian now; I wasn't when you came before.'

'Was it during the special week?' I asked.

'No,' he said, 'but that was when it all began.'

A girl aged eight from a Christian home, who came to Christ at camp, told me many years later that she waited a whole year before she felt ready to share the experience with an adult. She grew up a consistent follower of Jesus and eventually married a fine Christian young man who is now ordained. A happy-ever-after-story if you like and this is so often true for those who come to love the Lord during childhood years.

As a result of careful teaching about the importance of belonging, the response is often made like this. It is a happy event in the experience of the child, and often such a natural thing that adult questioning about its reality cannot help but be puzzling to the boy or girl.

I once read a story of a millionaire who, late at night, in the luxurious personal suite of one of his own hotels, had a sudden and simple longing for an apple. As it was late he decided to make his way to the hotel kitchens and get himself one. But he was disturbed in his search. He established his identity with some difficulty, and made known his quest. The kitchen and other staff were alerted, refrigerators and cupboards were unlocked and eventually a procession of waiters brought an elegant dish piled high with every kind of fruit to his apartment, together with china plates, silver knives and forks, and spotless table linen. He gazed at it all in dismay. 'My appetite has gone,' he said. 'All I wanted was an apple which I could cut, peel with my old pocket-knife, eat and enjoy all to myself. I don't want it any more.'

This is the kind of thing that happens when a child expresses a wish to belong to Jesus. There are fussy grown-ups with questions and more questions. 'Do you understand this?' 'Do you realize that?'

The child may well say, 'All I wanted to do was to say, "Yes" to Jesus. I don't think I want to any more.'

However, the importance of the children's conscious response to the Saviour must not be underrated.

'It is not enough to teach the gospel,' says John Stott in *Preacher's Portrait*. 'We must urge men to embrace it.' This is also true of boys and girls. In the introduction I quoted from the report entitled, 'Towards the conversion of England' which says, 'The definite call to decide for Christ should come to every child before the change from primary to secondary education.'

To encourage the personal response of the child is the proper responsibility of all dedicated parents and teachers. They will accept it as part of the commission which has been laid upon us by our Lord himself and will seek the help of the Holy Spirit for its urgent encouragement in order to bring it understandably and happily within the scope of the child's experience.

If the responsibility is to be adequately fulfilled there must also be some working knowledge of the theology of response and an awareness of its proper scriptural presentation to the individual, particularly to the child. With children especially in mind, there are four essentials which must now be considered.

1. The meaning of the heart of a child in the context of response.

2. The importance of 'Effectual calling' in the same context.

3. The proper use of biblical doctrine and illustration for the encouragement of response.

4. The importance of providing opportunity for response and the suitability of personal and group counselling.

The Heart of a Child

It has been said that at the heart of every human problem is the problem of the heart. A proper understanding of the biblical usage of this word will save us from many pitfalls and the children from considerable confusion. More religious nonsense is talked about the heart than any other biblical subject. Our English word 'heart' translates quite literally the Greek *kardia* and its Hebrew equivalent in the Old Testament. It is a simple and lively metaphor to the adult mind. To the child who thinks literally it raises the kind of question asked, perhaps facetiously, by a twelve-year-old boy in a biology lesson, 'Please sir, which is the religious part?'

The child's confusion is increased when he is constantly presented with different coloured heart shaped silhouettes, one perhaps with a door in. These are visual aids to show the possible alternative states of his spiritual condition. Pictures of physical hearts may be all right for lovers, but are as unsuitable for teaching children as pictures of bowels or kidneys would be, though both of these are also used metaphorically in the Scriptures to describe the feelings and affections.

The use of a good concordance will soon reveal that in the Bible the heart of the man is the man *thinking* and *feeling* and *choosing*. The heart of the child is the child thinking with its mind, feeling with its emotions, and choosing with its will. It is the intelligent exercise of mind, affections and will. It may be a wayward heart, a rebellious heart, a hard heart. Or it may be a heart responding in faith to the Good News about Jesus.

First of all, though it may not be the first in conscious experience, there is the response of the mind. 'Faith comes from what is heard, and what is heard comes from the preaching of Christ' (Rom. 10:17) 'Men must grasp the truth before they are asked to respond to it.' (*Preacher's Portrait* by John Stott.).[1] The experience of evangelistic missions, whether for adults or children, is that those who properly respond are usually the ones who have a background of religious teaching however small. This is why a children's church-based mission should be concerned primarily with the children with whom the church is already in touch, while a holiday mission or club which caters mostly for untaught children, should press very cautiously for decisions. For both kinds of children all religious instruction should be based on the Bible and have a teaching content which by the Holy Spirit's application will appeal to the mind of the child.

Secondly, when preaching and teaching are in the power of the Holy Spirit, proper feelings, such as surprise, fear, sorrow, joy and love for Christ, will be aroused. These feelings are legitimate and necessary if there is to be a true response to Christ.

Finally there is the exercise of the will. 'Come down,' said Jesus to the surprised Zacchaeus, 'for today I must stay at your house.' And he came down and received Him joyfully.

These are the necessary components for believing with the heart — *thinking* about Jesus and His work intelligently, *feeling* about Him emotionally, and *choosing* to say Yes to Him determinedly.

The heart of an individual is the individual's PERSONALITY. An integrated personality is one in which mind, will and feelings are under proper control. A consecrated personality is one where mind, feelings and will are wholly yielded to God in Christ. It is legitimate to use the word *life* instead of heart where it is allowed in the context of what is being said. For example, it is more understandable to a child to be encouraged to receive the Lord Jesus into his *life* rather into his *heart*. *Believing* with the heart is more easily understood.

The important thing is to use the word as the Bible uses it, and please, please, throw away all those heart-shaped pictures and models.

'What is Effectual Calling?' asks the Scottish shorter catechism. And the answer is, 'Effectual Calling is the work of God's Spirit, whereby convincing us of our sin and misery (i.e. the feelings), enlightening our minds in the knowledge of Christ (i.e. the mind), and renewing our wills (i.e. the will). He doth persuade and enable us to embrace

8

Jesus Christ freely offered to us in the Gospel.'

It is with the heart that the child, like the adult, believes unto Justification. And he who believes shall never be ashamed.

Effectual Calling

I want now to examine the importance of 'effectual calling' in the context of the response of a child.

Because the Gospel has been proclaimed to an audience it does not necessarily mean that every individual present will have heard the call of God to his mind and will and feelings. There is all the difference in the world between the outward and the inward call, the latter being a most necessary qualification for any intelligent and deliberate response by a child to God.

Dr James Packer says in *Evangelism and the Sovereignty of God*, 'We must learn to rest all our hopes of fruit in evangelism upon the omnipotent grace of God. For God does what man cannot do. God works by His Spirit through His Word in the hearts of sinful men to bring them to repentance and faith. Faith is a gift of God (Phil. 1:29; Eph. 2:8). So, too, repentance is the gift of God.'[3] (Acts 5:31; 11:18). He continues, 'Paul terms this God's work of calling' (1 Cor. 1:26; Eph. 1:18; 4:4; 2 Tim. 1:9 etc.). The old theologians called it effectual calling to distinguish it from the ineffective summons that is given when the gospel is preached to a man in whose heart God is not at work. It is the operation whereby God causes sinners to understand and respond to the gospel invitation ... It is thus a calling that creates the response which it seeks, and confers the blessing to which it invites.'[4] The Westminster Confession describes this 'effectual calling' as follows: 'An activity of God in and upon fallen men enlightening their minds spiritually and savingly to understand the things of God; taking away the heart of stone, and giving unto them a heart of flesh; and renewing their wills, and by his almighty power determining them to that which is good; and effectually drawing them to Jesus Christ; yet so as they come most freely, being made willing by His grace.'

William Temple says, 'Our action is all response; all initiative is with the Lord; not ye chose me, but I chose you.' [5]

For some the calling will be dramatic and critical. For others there will be no conscious moment of calling. Experience shows it to be God's work from start to finish, covering all the ages of childhood.

Ideally the calling will come to the children through the teaching of their parents at home. It will also come through our example, through the teaching of the Word of God and often through a children's mission in the church. The evidence of the calling will be in the illuminating of the mind, the stirring of the feelings and the renewing of the will. Without such a calling, made possible by the sovereign work of God, there can be no appropriate response from the heart of the child. In such a calling the Godhead finds expression, for it is the responsibility of the Father, by the constraining love of Christ, brought about through the work of the Holy Spirit. This all-important truth must ever be borne in mind by both parents and workers alike as it will eliminate the use of any form of unfair adult personality appeal or high pressure performance. We must, however, play our part, by teaching the Scriptures, prayerfully, clearly, lovingly and urgently and by believing in the faithfulness of God to direct the word to the heart of the listener. It is true that there are those who have made their conscious response after hearing just one verse of scripture or just one children's talk or simply through the influence of Christian friends. But experience shows that an effectual call comes usually through the regular teaching of the Holy Scriptures and by the power of the Holy Spirit. An intelligent eleven-year-old boy said to me recently at camp, 'Your talks have been very helpful to me. Being a choirboy I have never been able to go to Sunday school and I've learnt a lot that I needed to know.'

We turn now to the third essential for a fulfilled ministry.

The Proper Use of Bible Doctrine and Illustration

There are many excellent, carefully-planned courses of Bible teaching for children. There are graded syllabuses catering for each of the age groups with which we shall be concerned. We must select such a course wisely bearing in mind its value and its suitability for our particular children.

It is a fair criticism that those who write these courses do so for children who are reasonably intelligent and come from the better housing areas, while the children from rougher homes and districts are far too easily forgotten. However, it is usually possible to adapt the material provided by writers who are dedicated men and women writing for the widest possible range of children.

For all the children there must be a comprehensively planned pattern of teaching of the essential Bible themes. The discipline of a two or three year syllabus is the only safeguard against repetition of favourite, well-worn passages, and a constant reiteration of the 'Come to Jesus' theme. The writer of Psalm 78 encourages us to expect that the children in our care will set their hope in God, and not forget his works but keep his commandments. (Ps. 78:7) The Psalmist by implication lays the responsibility primarily upon the parents and parent-substitutes and says, 'Tell to the coming generation the glorious deeds of the Lord, and his might, and the wonders which he has wrought' (Ps. 78:4).

The response of the children in verse 7 is entirely dependent upon the faithful teaching fulfilment of verse 4, which also provides us with a pattern for our own instructional themes. Our teaching is to be ALL ABOUT GOD AND ALL ABOUT JESUS.

At the commencement of every children's mission or camp I find it necessary to explain and emphasize the reality of God and his character, the historicity and uniqueness of Jesus and the reliability of the Scriptures.

The teaching given to the children in many churches and Sunday schools often includes excellent material concerning the person and ministry of Christ but has little to say about the character and holiness of God. Yet it is essential that children be taught about God, not only that they might learn, but also to prepare them for the humanistic and atheistic onslaught that will undoubtedly attack them in the later years at school. So good teaching is necessary in the early years. Young children must be shown that God is real and wonderful, that he is Life and Light and Love, and cares about each of us personally. The teaching given about Jesus Christ and His relationship to the individual is often limited; sometimes nothing more than a repetition in one form or another of the statement, 'You are a sinner. Jesus died for you. You must repent and believe and you will be saved.'

Remember Paul's statement to the Corinthians at the beginning of the Epistle, 'I decided to know nothing among you except Jesus Christ and Him crucified.' (1 Cor. 2:2) This did not prevent him from writing glorious things about the living Lord Jesus at the end of the very same letter. We can read them in Chapter 15. Certainly we must tell the children that Jesus died. We must also follow the example of Paul and other writers in the New Testament and tell them of the wonderful things about the living Lord Jesus who is longing to be a present friend and helper. Such teaching is more relevant to children than that of forgiveness for the past, or going to heaven in the future. They want to know of Christ's promised presence in their lives. They are eager to learn of Christ's love, his power, his promise of guidance and of his strength and availability. We must also constantly underline the Deity of Christ and point to his manifestation in the flesh as a revelation of the person and character of God the Father.

It is beyond the scope of this book to provide any detailed syllabus for children's lessons. All I can do now is to point out some of the pitfalls which are likely to occur in their presentation.

We must always remember that children are literalists who are often puzzled by the use of metaphor or simile whether it be Biblical or otherwise.

It is not easy to explain to younger children the meaning of many of the profound statements of Jesus, as, when showing Himself to be the giver of eternal life, he spoke of himself as 'Bread' and 'Water'. The metaphor of 'Light' is easier to explain, whilst the illustration of the Good Shepherd and the sheep is so easy to understand it can be enjoyed by the youngest child. So we must be careful how we select our Bible themes and illustrations. The standard list of children's talks probably needs much wider revision than is readily realized.

Doors are a difficulty. Sometimes the child is presented with a visual door which he is invited to enter. This is based on the statement of Jesus, 'I am the door; if anyone enters by me, he will be saved.' (John 10:9) Good material for a visual aid, it is far from easy to turn into understandable teaching. The confusion is made worse when the child is subsequently shown another door which he is invited to open. The invitation is based on the appeal of Revelation 3:20 'Behold I stand at the door and knock; if anyone hears my voice and opens the door, I will come in to him and eat with him and he with me.' This verse (though taken out of its context) is such a popular text for inviting response that I shall probably be shouted down when I plead for its sparing use on the grounds that it is an adult metaphorical concept difficult for children to understand.

It is much better to use a literal account of the response of Zacchaeus for example, who welcomed Jesus joyfully into his home and into his life. Verses 1 to 10 of Luke 19 provide one of the most understandable accounts of literal response recorded in the New Testament. They show so vividly how Jesus faced an individual with the unhappy consequences of his wrongdoings and rewarded his response with forgiveness, friendship and salvation. It seems a great pity that this illustration of a desperately needy individual's response has been frivolously turned into a nursery rhyme, tea-party happening by a popular children's chorus.

Probably the best example of *entering a door* as distinct from *opening a door* as an illustration of response is the Old Testament record of Noah and his family entering the ark. Here again we have a literal happening and it is possible to show to the older children the meaning of the ark as a picture of Christ.

We must also beware of the danger of using gimmicks. Recently, I discovered in America a fellowship of 'Christian magicians' and a magazine about gospel conjuring. One suggestion was for the speaker to place a piece of red silk inside a box, close it, open it again and hey presto, the silk was white. You do not need me to explain the application. There were many such pieces of apparatus used and many similar routines. One of the more skilful exponents of the art advertised his meetings as 'Gospel entertainment'. It is possible that this kind of gospel application is already being used in the British Isles, yet it is so extremely dangerous.

First, it links the Holy Spirit's change of heart and life with trickery and unreality. Secondly, the children are confused by what amounts to a double metaphor in almost every performance. The magical apparatus is usually an illustration of a metaphor, both of which have to be explained. In the example given sins like scarlet are made as white as snow.

Thirdly, the children all the time are likely to be working out how it is done, no doubt enjoying the entertainment but skilfully switching off for the application.

'Curioser and curioser,' said Alice as she became more and more involved in Lewis Carroll's Wonderland. She was none the wiser when she woke up again at the end of the story. So it is better for us to avoid the type of approach in which red liquids turn to white, or aircraft, space rockets or vacuum cleaners feature. Unless of course they are simple supporting illustrations. Such talks may be entertaining but are extremely difficult for a child to understand. Biblical material is always best and there is more than enough for all.

Undoubtedly there is a place and time for a lighter side in our dealings with the children. This will help us to build and use the important bridge of friendship. But anything likely to sidetrack from the real issue, or subtract from the sacredness of our ministry, must be strictly avoided. Music and drama both have a potential for good in our endeavour to reach the children, though misuse or overuse can be dangerous and distracting.

Having avoided the pitfalls, provided regular courses of straightforward Bible teaching, and recognized the necessity of the 'Effectual Call' by the Holy Spirit to the heart of the child, we are still left with the wise words of John Stott already quoted, 'It is not enough to teach the Gospel; we must urge men to embrace it.'

The final consideration of this chapter, is therefore concerned with the importance of providing opportunities for response together with the suitability and manner of counselling.

The Importance of Providing Opportunity for Response

From time to time, during the regular course of teaching in church and Sunday school, the question of conscious response and renewal will inevitably crop up. Opportunity must therefore be provided for this. Some churches set aside an annual Sunday with this in mind; others hold regular missions every two or three years, with follow-up visits by a carefully chosen missioner who becomes known and trusted by the children.

This kind of activity forms the greater part of my own ministry and I can speak from experience of its spiritual fruitfulness, especially when the children who attend the meetings have a background of previous faithful teaching. An annual church children's camp providing residential experiences in a truly Christian environment is extremely valuable, and indeed essential for the spiritual well-being of children from non-Christian families. In their different ways these will provide opportunities to show the children not only how they may come to the Saviour for themselves, but also how their relationships with him may be renewed and strengthened. Remember that when a child responds to Christ, or seeks a renewal of such a response, there must be as little adult interference as possible to allow the Holy Spirit to work in the young life.

After many years of thought and careful observation, I am

more than ever convinced that during a mission, camp or on a special Sunday, the ideal time for the invitation to be given is at the end of the meeting when all the children are still there. During the final days of a mission there may be a number of occasions when, after the talk has been given, there is time for quiet personal response. It is more than likely, however, that there will be a special 'Way talk' which will show how the response can be made, and emphasize its importance. This will be followed by a short time of quiet for individual prayer. There will be no build up of tension, and the invitation will be given clearly to the children to say 'Yes' to Jesus for themselves, for the first time or in a new and realistic way. It is important always for both kinds of response to be presented together.

In special cases where numbers are unwieldy or where there are restless or unruly children, the 'Way meeting' may need to be organized separately for those who are concerned and who are prepared to take it seriously. At such a time it may be expected that many children will hear the call of God inwardly in their hearts and respond. But there must be no button-holing or loaded-questioning of individuals by over-keen younger inexperienced helpers. The boys and girls can be encouraged to ask questions and there can be a hand-out 'Way' booklet or letter with a printed response prayer. Better still, the children may be told that this is available for those who wish if they will ask or perhaps write for a copy. The letter to be posted in a special letter box can also list the events of the activity which have been liked or disliked. Alternatively, the child may simply write on a blank card, 'booklet please' or, 'letter please', with his name and age. The missioner may also feel it to be helpful to invite the children to tell him in their letter if they have said 'yes' to Jesus with an assurance that this will be a secret between them and him. He may say, 'It is more than likely that you have loved the Lord Jesus for as long as you can remember, and you have now said a special Yes to him. Or, it may be that you have never really thought about it before but now you too want to say Yes. Or some of you who are older may have begun to say

No, and you want to turn round and say Yes instead. When we pray in a moment just quietly tell God. Later on, if you feel it would help, ask for or write for one of the booklets. It might also help you to tell me (or write to me) privately that you have said Yes in this special way.'

For some children the happening is too real and sacred to share with anyone for the time being; for others it can be helpful to tell someone who can really be trusted. It is important for the children to understand that their declaration of response is confidential. We shall know in the days to come whether they are sincere or not, for it will be seen in their lives.

The missioner must never give in to the temptation of quoting numbers when speaking of the children who have responded.

The card or leaflet used will need to be carefully chosen, and must avoid putting words into the children's minds.

It is important also to approach the children as if they already loved the Lord. In Canada a Christian mother told me how her daughter, aged nine or ten, came home weeping from a children's mission. When asked why she was crying she replied, 'I don't like that man; he makes me feel I don't belong to Jesus, and I do.' I do not know who the missioner was. All too often this is the impression that children get from what is said because the speaker has approached them as if all of them were outside the kingdom. How much better if he were to say, 'It is more than likely that you have loved the Lord Jesus for as long as you can remember. If so, I want to help you to know him better. If not, I want to show you how to begin.'

It is encouraging when children write or say, 'I have loved Jesus for as long as I can remember,' or 'I became a Christian when I was six or seven, but I now understand a lot better than I did.' It is encouraging too when children are seen growing up happily in the church as true disciples of Jesus and readily declaring their faith by joining the church when the opportunity arises. We should do well to consider here the popular methods of counselling. These are fraught with danger for adults and are certainly unsuitable for children. An adult or perhaps an inexperienced teenager, armed with a large Bible and a set of texts and questions sits by a child and persuades him to 'make a decision for Christ.'

Such activity is most unsuitable for children because:

1. It is adult in concept and performance. Even when an attempt has been made to adapt it to boys and girls, it is an unnatural, forced approach for the encouragement of child response. Inevitably its high pressure structure is likely to arouse resentment and suspicion in the minds of parents.

2. It is far removed from our Lord's own bidding, 'Let the children come to me, and do not hinder them.' We are to be concerned for their coming. By all proper means we are to make it possible for them to come and to show them how to do so. We are to encourage them to come. But we may not cajole, coerce, entice, goad, bewitch, provoke, frighten, bribe, or even persuade. Compulsion and conviction are the prerogatives of the Holy Spirit. In our encouragement of the children to respond, we must carefully avoid any usurping of the ministry which belongs to God himself.

3. Leading a child to Christ requires experience and dedication. Rarely are there sufficient counsellors of such calibre to go round, even when the children are organized in pairs or groups.

4. For a child, it turns a natural, simple and beautiful event into a complicated performance. Oh! the questions asked; 'What is your name?' 'How old are you?' 'Where do you live?' 'Do you belong to this church, this club, this Sunday school?' The counsellor insists on writing it all down. And this is only the beginning. After this comes the Bible interrogation. Is it any wonder that the child is bewildered and confused? By its very nature the procedure is likely to evoke a response which is from the head and not the heart. The argument leaves no loophole for contradiction and produces assent though rarely conviction.

Experience shows that the consequent lists of children who have made a decision are usually completely meaningless. Because of this the cause of children's evangelism is discredited. Sceptics in the church say, 'I told you so.' The children themselves, finding nothing has happened after all, are disillusioned and may become scornful, cynical — even contemptuous. It is very much better, giving every opportunity for the asking and answering of questions, to show the way in the meeting and to entrust the children to the care of the Holy Spirit.

Regularly during a mission I will say to the children as the meeting finishes, 'This evening, instead of going to the door to say "Good Night" to you all, I shall stay at this end of the church and sit on my tall stool. If anyone has a question, come and talk to me.' Usually a number of children will come, asking all kinds of questions. To begin with, the questions are often completely secular, developing, as confidence grows, into the sharing of personal problems and unhappinesses. There may be questions too about the evening's talk and programme. As far as is possible all questions are answered on the spot, or else, if the question is a serious one and requires more than a spot answer, the opportunity is made for the child to have a less hurried and more private talk.

From time to time there is likely to be a child in the group who has a real sense of need, maybe with a conviction of wrongdoing. It is then important to go very gently and sensitively, meeting the child always at the point of his present conscious need. We cannot expect to solve every child's problem with the routine 'Come to Jesus' syndrome. There can be no stereotyped pattern and certainly no substitute for experience, for this is specialist work.

It is always better to talk to a single child or a group of children in the surroundings where you happen to be at the time and not to take them off to some separate, often dingy and unattractive room set aside for this special purpose. The more natural and relaxed we can be in our personal work the better. When talking to children, sit, even if on the floor. Use a small Bible and always take the children seriously. Be happy, natural, relaxed and prayerful but never flippant. Follow the example of our Lord who met individuals at the point of their own special need. I remember, as a young and earnest worker, asking some children during an after-meeting in a poorer district of Birmingham why they felt they needed to come to Jesus? And being shocked and puzzled when a girl replied, 'Please sir, my Dad's in the army.' I realize now, of course, that with her father constantly away from the family her immediate need was for the friendship and love of Jesus, and upon that need I should have encouraged her to come to the Saviour. Instead, I quite wrongly followed my own stereotyped pattern and spoke of wrongdoing and the need of forgiveness and regeneration.

In our dealing with children we must always remember to respect their confidence. Not only what may be written in a letter, but also what may be said. I have learnt that anything a child passes on to a parent or a worker regarding his response to the Saviour, or anything else for that matter, should be treated as being absolutely confidential. The children should be made aware of this.

A parent may say, 'Can I tell Daddy?' or, 'Mummy?' as the case may be. Or a leader may ask permission to share the confidence with his opposite number. It is always dangerous for a child's confession of faith to be made known to all the realatives, or to the people at the local church or to become public property at the supermarket. Because a child instinctively knows that, by and large, adults cannot be trusted with his secrets and may use them as evidence against him, he becomes uncommunicative. A parent is fortunate if his children, knowing he can be trusted, share their sacred things with him.

The child himself may want brothers and sisters to know that he has made this special response to Jesus, particularly if he is in a Christian family. However, the faith of a child is a sacred and precious thing, not to be tarnished by being bandied around, probed into and betrayed.

By the same token it is a mistake to teach children that they should tell someone that they have come to Jesus, on the basis of Romans 10:9. This is an adult concept which the child will appreciate later on. His immediate need is to be shown the importance of witness and testimony by changed behaviour, and by letting his light shine. If a real work of the Holy Spirit has taken place it will become increasingly obvious in all kinds of ways both in the church and in the home. As the child grows older he will be shown the importance of being ready to give an audible answer to those who may ask him why he is different now. But we must be very patient with a child's inconsistencies, always remembering our own. We must not expect too much, too soon.

The Most Difficult Question of them All

'I want to say "Yes" to Jesus,' or 'I want to let Jesus come into my life. *But how can I?*'

This is the question constantly asked by thinking boys and girls who have heard the call of God to come to him. It is the crux of the whole problem and it would seem to be still unanswered in what I have already said. Basically, of course, the question can be answered only by the promised enlightening of the Holy Spirit. As parents and teachers, however, we are likely to be the channels through whom the enlightening comes, and we must be those who are informed regarding both the theology and its presentation.

In the pursuit of my own evangelistic activities with children for many years, the ability to provide a truly satisfactory answer to this question has been constantly in my thinking. In the early days I used the illustration of a small boy jumping through a trap-door into the arms of his father who was standing in a darkened room below and encouraging him to make the leap of faith. There was a commonly-used illustration of crossing a bridge, and another telling of the difference between believing *about* a chair and believing *in* the chair by sitting on it. We used the opening of a door, based on the declaration of Revelation 3:20, and the picture, 'The Light of the World' to illustrate our theme; and there were many more. But in recent years I have come to realize, more than ever before, that such illustrations do not go far enough in the answering of this critical question. And I have come to appreciate the straight-forward clarity of the scriptural declaration recorded in John 1:12, 'But to all who received him, who believed in his name, he gave power to become children of God.'

I have come to see that receiving and believing are complementary and should rarely, if ever, be presented in isolation. It is always receiving and being received. It is an active two way response — I receive Jesus who comes to me and he receives me as I believe on his name and come to him. So it is that the individual and the Saviour come to belong to one another, and the individual becomes a child of God.

Response must always be presented in this way, reciprocally, personally. We forget too easily that it is impossible to have faith in a vacuum. It is the faith of a person in a person, of the sinner in the Saviour. It is his love for me and my love for him. In this simple form it really does appear to be acceptable to the children themselves. I have sought to develop this theme in my children's booklet, 'Belonging'. God and Jesus say 'Yes' to the individual whilst the individual says 'Yes' to them. Always in that order. 'You did not choose me' Jesus reminded His disciples, 'but I chose you' (John 15:16).

An explanation of John 1:12 is probably the best answer we can give to the enquiring child: 'To all who received Him, who believed in His name, He gave the power to become children of God.' This wonderful scripture can be developed in numerous ways.

I remember once listening to Dr John Laird speaking to children about this. First he placed his hands one above the other. Beginning with the lower hand he used the thumb and fingers to spell out the word F-A-I-T-H. Then using the thumb and fingers of the top hand he spelt out the word J-E-S-U-S.

'It is my F-A-I-T-H in J-E-S-U-S,' he said. Then bringing his hands together, palms facing, fingers interlocking, he added 'Jesus comes to me and I come to him. We come to belong to one another.' This is a true and beautiful illustration of receiving and being received.

In the same context I will never forget overhearing the prayer of a ten-year-old boy during a C.S.S.M. Beach Mission in Scotland many years ago. 'Please Lord Jesus', he said, 'I want you to receive me into your heart. And I want to receive you into my heart. And I want it to happen now. Amen.'

I often use the illustration of a man and woman getting married. Each says, 'I will' to the other and the promise is sealed with the giving and receiving of a ring. Each enters the other's life and they belong to one another.

Another vivid illustration of this is the Old Testament experience of Jacob at Bethel. Significantly, without a word about his wrongdoing, the substance of what Jacob heard God say to him in his dream was, 'Jacob I have been the friend of your grandfather Abraham, and the friend of your father Isaac, and I want to be your friend too.' In response to this when Jacob woke up he poured the oil on the stone and declared, 'The Lord shall be my God.' The oil on the stone, like the ring on the finger, set the seal on the promise. 'The Lord shall be my God, AND I REALLY MEAN IT.' For Jacob this was the moment of conscious and personal belonging, the beginning of a new way of life. Here are two quotations concerning the response of a child to Christ which have been meaningful to me in my own work for many years. The first is a poem written by a friend and neighbour Fay Inchfawn who has kindly given me persmission to use it here.[7]

Say not it is an easy thing
To lead a little child to Christ.
Say rather that the circumstance demands
A humble lifting up of cleansed hands.
'Elisha ... stretched himself upon the child.'
And shall I come defiled
To this most holy task? Or weakly dare
To shelve the Godly exercise of prayer?
To think, by anecdote, or fable,
Or some such feeble thing,

To capture child-soul for its rightful King?
Lord, teach me, even me.
So shall I meekly learn that only he
Who will expend the utmost he receives
Shall come at last rejoicing
Bringing in the sheaves.

The second is from the writings of George Goodman comparing the day-school teacher with the Sunday-school teacher. 'The lecturer and day-school teacher have as their first aim the imparting of knowledge; the Sunday-school teacher or speaker has it as his first aim to *introduce his hearers to a living Person,* even the Lord Jesus Christ. The lecturer can do his work by natural means, the Christian worker needs divine and supernatural help. He can only do his work by the Holy Spirit, and is therefore helpless unless his work is accomplished by a holy life, a godly walk and much prayer.'[8]

Finally, we must always include the children in our prayers, particularly with regard to their response to the Saviour. And we must always be willing to teach them as the opportunity arises. This cannot help but bring its own reward. We must remember that the Lord Himself knows who are His. Their salvation belongs to Him from beginning to end.

Chapter Eight

THE AGE OF ACCOUNTABILITY

'When the child knows how to refuse the evil and choose the good' Isaiah 7:15–16. In Chapter One I quoted Dr Griffith Thomas as follows, 'Children are born with an evil nature in a state of what is called depravity, and when reason dawns they know something of right and wrong, though they have only a partial responsibility, but in course of time they become fully responsible for the sin of their own will.' The time of a child becoming fully responsible, is the moment of spiritual discretion or accountability.

Dr Thomas continues, 'Surely the truth is that all children are included in the great atoning sacrifice and belong to Jesus Christ until they deliberately refuse Him.' This basic fact, which is essential for a proper understanding of a child's response, has been constantly underlined throughout this book. Until this moment of conscious reponse has been reached in the life and experience of a child, he is a 'not-yet-unbeliever' just as he is a 'not-yet-believer' in the biblical sense of conscious, intelligent, heart belief towards our Lord and his atoning work.

If when the time of accountability is reached, the child then rejects the truth, he comes under the judgment of God. More happily, if the child responds to the call of the Holy Spirit and comes to the light, it will be clearly seen in his life and deeds — See John 3:16–21.

Any attempt to pinpoint a moment in the life of a child as being the actual age of accountability will be met with disappointment.

Children are so unpredictable and different from each other

that there cannot be a norm. Their behaviour spectrum is far too wide. All we can do is to take specimen patterns of answerable behaviour and use them wisely and expectantly for each individual child. The law of course, lays down a workable schedule of age responsibilities. As we consider the age of spiritual accountability it may be helpful to take note of this..

At the time of writing (1974) the law has changed the age of criminal responsibility from eight to twelve years old. After a period of report and observation it may be further changed to thirteen or fourteen years.

Consent for a surgical operation can be given at 16. A blood donor must be 18. Parents have maintenance obligations to their children until the age of 21 and in most cases this age has also to be reached for the inheritance of an estate. It is still not possible to become a Member of Parliament until 21. The wide range of age in the development of children also helps us to appreciate the difficulties of any measurement of responsibility in terms of time.

Parents constantly complain that their children grow up too quickly, and it is certainly true that physiological development has been taking place earlier. In 1960 it was reckoned that the average ten-year-old, in every anatomical and physiological sense, was the same as the average eleven-year-old in 1900. The trend has continued, though obviously it cannot go on forever!

A child's emotional attitudes are thought to bear some relation to physiological events. It seems reasonable to suppose that the physical development of our children is likely to have some bearing on the exercising of their conscious spiritual response, and that today this too may be expected to occur earlier, rather than later. We should also remember that the age of physical development in girls is usually ahead of boys, roughly two weeks at birth and gradually increasing to two years ahead at adolescence. This also may have a bearing on the tendency for girls to make a conscious spiritual response at a younger age than boys.

My own knowledge of this is based on observation rather than statistics.

The age of the first menstrual period for girls can be as early as ten or as late as sixteen. For boys the beginning of testes growth can be as early as ten or as late as thirteen, whilst quicker growth may start anywhere between ten and sixteen. There can be considerable age differences for development among children of the same family, even between un-identical twins. All this must be borne in mind when we consider the age of spiritual accountability. The variations will probably apply here too, even with members of the same family.

Some children then are slower starters in growing-up, in acting independently, and in their understanding of things. So we must not be surprised if some are also slow starters in their spiritual response to the Saviour or indeed if boys are slower than girls in making their decision. We must not be discouraged about this, for it does not necessarily mean that nothing is happening in these lives. God is always in control of the situation. It is with this in mind that parents and teachers are constantly asking if there is any indication from either the Bible or experience as to when the age of accountability is likely to be reached.

Age Four

A highly intelligent titled lady who organized Sunday services for children in her Kensington flat which I used to visit, said to me on one occasion, 'I first came to put my trust in Jesus when I was four though I cannot remember the time when I did not love Him.'

Age Seventeen

I recall an incident related by Mr Hudson Pope who was a dedicated children's evangelist for the greater part of his life. The incident concerned a boy of seventeen who readily came to the Saviour at the conclusion of a meeting. 'As he was leaving,' Mr Pope said, 'I asked him why he had not come to Christ before.' The boy replied, 'Sir, I had never heard it before.'

The age of accountability for the girl was four but for this particular boy it was seventeen.

Age Twenty

The children of Israel who were not to be allowed into the Promised Land because of their unbelief were 'twenty years old and upward'. (Numbers 14:28–32)

The Roman Centurion

Undoubtedly the most vivid example in the New Testament is Cornelius who made an immediate response to the Holy Spirit's revelation concerning Jesus. Though he may have known about Jesus historically, until that moment there was no inward appreciation or understanding. He was neither a believer nor an unbeliever but, by force of ignorance and circumstance, a non-believer or a not-yet-believer.

This kind of deferred adult accountability, though probably rare, is still perpetuated in the experience of those, even in our own land, who grow up 'fearing God and doing what is right' (Acts 10:35) They have not heard the Good News concerning the way properly and scripturally proclaimed and they walk according to the light they possess. Regarding these, as Peter declared to Cornelius, 'In every nation anyone who fears God and does what is right is acceptable to Him.'

Commenting on this Dr Campbell Morgan says: 'The apostle did not mean to say that man is received upon the basis of his morality. God has cleansed, and God's reception of the race is based upon the passion of God, as wrought out in the Cross, according to this great evangel. But no man is to be saved because he understands the doctrine of the Atonement. He is saved, not by understanding it, but because he fears God and works righteousness. Oh, the glad and glorious surprise of those ultimate days when we find that there will be those who walked in the light they had, and wrought righteousness, and were acceptable to Him; not because of their morality, but by the infinite merit of the Cross, and by the fact that they yielded themselves to the light they possessed. The sin of the Gentile is not that he does not believe the thing of which he has never heard. It is that he holds down the truth which he knows, in unrighteousness.'[1]

For Cornelius then as for many others who have long since passed childhood, the preaching of the Good News concerning Jesus and the accompanying conviction of the Holy Spirit comes later in life. This for them is the moment of accountability. (Acts 10:34–48)

With all these examples in mind it is evident that there can be no fixed age of accountability. Experience shows, however, that the moment of deliberate and conscious response for children brought up in the discipline and instruction of the Lord, is most likely to be somewhere between the ages of seven and eleven. These are the golden years of childhood; the habit-forming years, when memory and discovery are active. Opportunities for teaching, training and all kinds of response are tremendous.

In this vulnerable period the mind, will, emotions – indeed the whole personality of the child – must be regarded as a sacred trust by those who have the opportunity to influence the young life.

It is true that some children are less demonstrative than others. Sometimes a child will seek to hide his true feelings behind a façade of affected indifference or even rebellion, being justifiably afraid of fuss or publicity. Yet it is very unlikely that a child from a truly Christian family will not have said 'Yes' consciously to the Saviour by the age of ten or eleven.

During puberty and adolescence some, though by no means all, will undergo a period of apparent uncertainty and sullen unresponsiveness even after years of happy childhood witness. Usually this is simply an expression of the traumatic experience of physical and emotional change. We must not write them off at this time for they need love, prayer, trust, and unending patience and care.

If the Lord himself has begun his work in the hearts and lives of our sons and daughters during childhood years, and they have responded to his love, we may trust them prayerfully to him for the completion of his gracious work. 'I am sure,' said Paul, 'that he who began a good work in you will bring it to completion at the day of Jesus Christ' (Phil. 1:6). As we rest our own perseverence on this tremendous promise, we may do the same for our children.

At the risk of being repetitive I must underline once more that the moment of conscious response on the part of the child, which he may look upon as the date of his becoming a Christian or becoming converted, is not likely to be the date when this actually happened and when the sovereign regenerating work of the Holy Spirit was done. It may be helpful for the child to have a date to look back upon, but it is essential for parents and workers to remember the Godward side of the total happening. This is the only real safeguard against the dangerous practice of dividing children into sheep and goats – those who belong and those who do not.

Conscious response will certainly reveal a boy or girl who really belongs to Christ. But this may be equally true for other children who are not yet aware of the necessity for an outward declaration. For children from non-Christian families, the ages of ten and upwards are critical ones indeed, particularly from ten to twelve. Because of the security needed, the child from a non-Christian home who has really come to Christ may well be a more forthright Christian in the church and Sunday school than the boy or girl from a Christian family.

Conversely, this is the time when we are likely to see children from non-Christian families who have refused the light leaving us altogether. This is happening today at an even younger age level and children of nine and ten are taunting their contemporaries for going to church and Sunday school.

Children are engaging in acts of violence and theft and

setting themselves deliberately in the ways of wrongdoing. at an increasingly early age. This also has to do with accountability. The important thing for all of us who truly love the Lord is to care, and to do all in our power to gather the children under the regular sound of the Good News and to make sure that it is faithfully taught and proclaimed in order that they may have the opportunity to hear the call of the Holy Spirit to come to the light. As we regularly engage in our spiritual ministry among the children let us never lose sight of the solemnity of our calling. Though there can be no specific age of discretion, we must remember that at any time our teaching may be used by God to bring some of our listeners into this very state of accountability, and to the point where some may deliberately say 'No' instead of 'Yes'. Paul reminds us, 'We are the aroma of Christ to God among those who are being saved and among those who are perishing, to one a fragrance from death to death, to the other a fragrance from life to life.' And he asks: 'Who is sufficient for these things?'

As we seek to fulfil the charge of our wonderful Lord Jesus to let the children come to Him, let us encourage ourselves by constantly remembering that our sufficiency is of God, and of God alone (2 Cor. 2:14–17).

Appendix

Introduction
1. From *The Prophet* by Kahil Gilbran.
2. *Towards the Conversion of England*, p. 88, The Press and Publications Board of the Church Assembly, 1945.

Chapter One CHILD STATUS
1. David Kingdon, writing as a Reformed Baptist says, 'We treat children as if they were unconverted until we are satisfied that they are.' 'Children of Abraham, A reformed Baptist View of Baptism', *The Covenant and Children* by David Kingdon, Henry E. Walter Ltd. and Carey Publications Ltd., 1973, p. 99. It should be realized, however, that this attitude is by no means held by all members of Baptist churches.
2. The Reverend John Pridmore.
3. *The Crises of the Christ* by G. Campbell Morgan, D.D., Pickering and Inglis Ltd. by permission.
4. Calvin Institutes, XVI, 17, 18, 20.
5. Compare Ireneus writing in the first century, 'Christ came to redeem all by Himself; all who through Him are regenerated to God; infants and little children, and young men, and older persons. Hence He passed through every age, and for the infants He became an infant, sanctifying infants; among the little children He became a little child, sanctifying those who belong to this age; and, at the same time, presenting them an example of well doing and obedience; among the young men He became a young man, that He might set them an example, and sanctify them to the Lord.'
6. See *Christian Nurture* by Horace Bushnell, D.D., Alexander Strahan and Sampson Low, Son, and Marston, 1866, p. 105 ff.
7. *The Biblical Doctrine of Infant Baptism*, by Pierre Ch. Marcel, translated from the French by Philip Edgcumbe Hughes, James

Clark & Co. Ltd., 1953, p. 117.

8. Bushnell *ut supra* pp. 74–75.

9. Compare the statements in Acts Chapters 10 and 11 concerning Cornelius who was a God-fearing man, with no proper knowledge of Christ or the Gospel. Yet he was acceptable to God. Particularly notice Acts 10:34–35. This grown man was never an unbeliever but by reason of ignorance he was a not-yet-believer.

10. *The Principles of Theology*, by W. H. Griffith Thomas, D.D., Longmans Green & Co., 1930, p. 158.

11. Ibid., p. 159.

12. Ibid., pp. 166–167. The quotation from Litten is provided to support Griffith Thomas' own statements regarding the condemnation in the Article of original sin as follows, 'And therefore in every person born into this world it (i.e. the sin not the individual) deserveth God's wrath and damnation.' Dr Thomas' own statement will repay careful study. The full quotation from Litton is as follows: 'Is it not, in fact, the nature and not the person that is regarded in all such statements? Sin may be considered abstractedly from the person in whom it resides: in its own nature it is *amartia*, or a missing of the mark, and *anomia* or contariety to the Divine law. In whomsoever, therefore, it is found, even as a latent potentiality it must *in itself* be an object of God's displeasure; but it does not follow that the person must be so, still less that the sentence on sin will in such a case be actually inflicted. The *fomes* or tendency, which if the infant lives will assuredly give birth to actual sin, cannot in God's sight be a thing indifferent; but as it is only an objective guiltiness (to which the will has not consented, because the subject is incapable of will), it may be covered from God's sight by an objective atonement (not appropriated by an act of will); so that the infant himself, if he dies as an infant, is not and never has been, an object of God's wrath.' Litton, *Introduction To Dogmatic Theology* (Second Edition), p162.

13. Griffith Thomas *ut supra*, p. 378.

14. *The Heathen Their Present State and Future Destiny* by George Goodman, Pickering & Inglis Ltd.

15. *Readings in St. John's Gospel* by William Temple, D.D., Macmillan & Co., 1952, p. 255.

16. See Genesis 17:9–14. Whether or not it is permissible to accept the Old Testament practice of circumcision as a parallel for infant baptism, it is interesting to notice that Abraham was instructed by Jehovah to circumcise not only the males born in his house but also those bought with his money who were not of his

offspring. The equivalent of adopted children were to be marked as sharers in the blessings of the covenant.

17. *The Righteous Judge*, by Harold E. Guillebaud, 1964, and *Life And Immortality* by Basil F. C. Atkinson, M.A., PhD., are both published privately and obtainable from Rev. Bernard Bateson, Winsham Vicarage, Chard, Somerset.

Chapter Two OF SUCH IS THE KINGDOM

1. *Daily Study Bible*, Rev. William Barclay, D.D., The Saint Andrew Press, The Gospel of Luke, p. 234.

2. Compare also Rom. 16:18; 1 Cor. 5:5–11; 16:18; 2 Cor. 12:5; 2 Thess. 3:12; 1 Tim. 6:5; Tit. 3:11; Philem. 9:3; 3 Jn. 8. Notice in the very few cases where the allusion is to those who are as the ones described it is always a literal, not an illustrative likeness.

3. Also compare David Kingdon in his recent book, *Children of Abraham* already quoted in Chapter One. Commenting on this statement of Jesus that 'to such belongs the kingdom of heaven', he writes, 'Is the thought here of literal children? Some think not.' R. E. O. White writes: 'As we have seen Jesus constantly addressed himself to the reason and conscience of adults, and so ought his followers. All three evangelists, on the evidence just given, plainly take the words to mean "of such as children is the kingdom of heaven" – the kingdom belongs to the *childlike*. Nothing is said of the relation of the child himself to the kingdom and to eternal life; but the incident is another priceless illustration of Jesus' attitude of love and gentleness, goodwill and prayerfulness, toward the child.' (R. E. O. White, *Baptism In The New Testament*).

David Kingdon continues, 'The difficulty with this view is that it ignores the force of the conjunction "for" or "because" (*gar*). It is a straining of language to make the Lord mean: "Let the children come to me, *for* the kingdom belongs to people who are like them, people who exhibit a childlike spirit." This is the more so since *toioutos* (of such as these) by no means implies the exclusion, but rather the inclusion, of the one mentioned. The child is one of the class it represents. When the Jews cried out against Paul (Acts 22:22), "Away with such a one!" (*toiouton*) they did not mean away with someone like Paul, but rather away with Paul and everyone like him (cf. Heb. 7:26 which says "For such (*toioutos*) an high priest became us" referring to our Lord who is unique). In the light of these examples our Lord must mean that the kingdom belongs to these children and all others like them.' (*Children of Abraham*, David Kingdon, Henry E. Walter Ltd. and Carey Publications Ltd., pp. 85–86).

In all fairness to David Kingdon who stresses his own position as a Reformed Baptist, it must be noted that he goes on to say: 'Before our Paedobaptist friends rejoice with great glee in what appears to be a capitulation to their position, it must be pointed out that there is not a word in the passage which would oblige us to restrict our Lord's statement to "covenant" children. He does not say that to "covenant" children belongs the kingdom of God, but to children without distinction. If all children are in view, and if infant baptism can be got out of this passage (which it can, only if it is first read in), then the text justifies the indiscriminate baptism of all infants, not the restriction of baptism to the children of believing parents' (ibid, p. 86). While it is sad to me and unnecessary to turn this into a denominational issue as an Anglican and Paedobaptist myself, I agree with Mr Kingdon's important analysis, and his showing that this is not strictly a 'covenant' text because, as I am also careful to show, it must be allowed to include the children of unbelieving parents as well as believing parents. I have dealt with the matter of indiscriminate baptism in Chapter One.

4. The statements in the Beatitudes concerning the kingdom of heaven are addressed to disciples to whom the kingdom belongs as their consolation not as their reward. As Edersheim is careful to point out, 'It is not *because* a man is poor in spirit that his is the kingdom of heaven, in the sense that one state will grow into the other, or be its result; still less is one the reward of the other. To adopt the language of St. Thomas Aquinas – it is neither *meritum ex congruo*, nor yet is it *ex condigno*. (The Reformers fully showed not only the error of Romanism in this respect, but the untenableness of the theological distinction).' Alfred Edersheim, M.A., D.D., Ph.D., *The Life and Times of the Messiah*, Longmans Green & Co., 1901, Vol. 1, p. 529.

5. *The Works and Words of Jesus*, by A. M. Hunter, B.D., Ph.D., D.Phil., S.C.M. Press, 1950.

6. *Life and Times of the Messiah*, ibid., Vol. 1, p. 270.

7. *The Mind Of Jesus*, by Rev. William Barclay, D.D., S.C.M. Press Ltd., 1960, p. 55.

8. *Works and Words of Jesus*, ibid., p. 72.

9. *Life and Times of the Messiah*, ibid., Vol. 1, p. 265.

10. *The Mind of Jesus*, ibid., p. 59.

11. *Works and Words of Jesus*, ibid., p. 76.

12. *Life and Times of the Messiah*, ibid., Vol. 1, p. 528.

13. *The Daily Study Bible* by Rev. William Barclay, D.D., Letter To The Hebrews, p. 8, and the Gospel of Matthew, p. 199.

14. Unpublished Lecture to Eclectics in Bristol by Canon J. Stafford Wright, M.A., by permission.

Chapter Three SOME ARE MORE PRIVILEGED

1. *Christian Nurture* by Horace Bushnell, D.D., Alexander Strahan and Sampson Low, Son and Marston, 1866, p. 4.

2. Bushnell, ibid., p. 7.

3. See also Psalm 107:41 and many Bible references to God's concern for the widow and the fatherless.

4. Bushnell, ibid., pp. 74–75.

5. Edwards, quoted by Bushnell, ibid., p. 20.

6. Bushnell, ibid., pp. 70–71.

7. Bushnell, ibid., p. 18.

8. Book of Common Prayer, Articles of Religion IX.

9. *Knots Untied*, by Rt. Rev. J. C. Ryle, D.D., William Hund & Co., 1874, p. 138.

10. *Outlines of Theology*, by Rev. A. A. Hodge, T. Nelson & Sons, 1872, p. 354.

11. Bushnell, ibid., pp. 50–51.

12. Compare L. Berkhof in *Systematic Theology*, The Banner of Truth Trust, pp. 471–472.

13. See Jeremiah 31:31–34; Hebrews 8:8–13.

14. See Romans 4:1–25; Galatians 3:7, 17, 26, 29; 4:21, 23, 28.

15. Compare David Kingdon who argues, 'that covenantal Paedobaptists should not be allowed to have the monopoly of covenant theology, since many Baptists both past and present have practised, and still practise, believers' baptism within the context of covenant theology.' And again, 'The second reason why the argument for infant baptism based on covenant theology continues to make such a strong appeal is because it takes seriously the unity of the Bible. Its starting point is that there is one covenant of grace which has been operative in human history since the Fall, the substance of which is the divine promise made to elect sinners, "I will be your God and you shall be my people". From the first disclosure of grace in the *protevangelium.* (Gen. 3:15) to the final vision of John the apostle, "Behold the tabernacle of God is with men, and He will dwell with them and be their God' (Rev. 21:3). Holy Scripture shows that there is but one covenant of grace

throughout all ages.' *Children of Abraham, A Reformed Baptist View of Baptism, The Covenant and Children*, by David Kingdon, Henry E. Walter Ltd. and Carey Publications Ltd., 1973, pp. 50 and 20.

16. *The Children for Christ*, by Rev. Andrew Murray, James Nisbet & Co. Ltd., 1905, p. 43.

17. Ibid., p. 71.

18. Ibid., p. 74.

19. *The Biblical Doctrine of Infant Baptism*, by Pierre Ch. Marcel, translated from the French by Philip Edgcumbe Hughes, James Clarke & Co. Ltd., 1953, p. 117.

20. Ibid., pp. 118–119.

21. Ibid., p. 107.

22. Ibid., p. 112.

Chapter Four THE UNDERPRIVILEGED CHILD

1. *Prayer*, by O. Hallesby, Inter Varsity Fellowship, 1953, p. 63.

2. 'Tell the Children How to Pray' from *Tell the Children*, 5, Hare Knapp, Bradford-on-Avon, Wiltshire.

Chapter Five THOSE WHO APPEAR TO SAY NO

1. *The Children for Christ*, by Rev. Andrew Murray, James Nisbet & Co. Ltd., 1905, p. 199.

2. *Lecture to Eclectics in Bristol*, by Canon J. Stafford Wright.

3. *Christian nurture*, by Horace Bushnell, D.D., Alexander Strahan and Sampson Low, Son and Marston, 1866, p. 75.

4. *The Daily Study Bible*, The Letter to the Hebrews, p. 12, The Rev. William Barclay, D.D., The Saint Andrew Press, Edinburgh.

5. *Beside The Bonnie Brier Bush*, by Ian Maclaren, Hodder & Stoughton, London.

6. *Lecture to Eclectics, ut supra*.

7. *Christian Nurture, ut supra*, pp. 29–30.

8. *Nature, Man and God*, William Temple (New York, The Macmillan Company, 1956), p. 243.

9. *The Four Loves*, by C. S. Lewis, Collins Fontana Books, 1963, p. 42.

10. *Christian Nurture, ut supra*, p. 75.

11. *Habitation of Dragons*, by Keith Miller, p. 141, Word Books London and Waco Texas, USA.

12. *Revivals of Religion*, by Charles Grandism Finney, Oliphants Ltd., 1928, p. 56.

13. *Revivals of Religion, ut supra*, p. 350.

Chapter Six SIN AND REPENTANCE

1. Book of Common Prayer, Article IX.

2. *The Heathen Their Present State And Future Destiny*, by George Goodman, Pickering & Inglis Ltd.

3. *The Principles of Theology*, by W. H. Griffith Thomas, D.D., Longmans Green & Co., 1930, p. 158.

4. Ibid, p. 166 ff.

5. Ibid., p. 378.

6. *Christian Nurture*, by Horace Bushnell, D.D., Alexander Strahan and Sampson Low, Son and Marston, 1866, pp. 4–5.

7. *The Mind of St. Paul*, by Rev. William Barclay, D.D., Collins Fontana, 1955, p. 36.

8. *The Dynamic of Service*, by A. Paget-Wilkes, Japan Evangelistic Band, 1955.

9. *Knots Untied*, by J. C. Ryle, D.D., 1901.

Chapter Seven THE RESPONSE OF THE CHILD

1. *The Preacher's Portrait*, by Rev. J. R. W. Stott, M.A., The Tyndale Press, 1961, p. 50.

2. Ibid., p. 48.

3. *Evangelism And The Sovereignty of God*, by Rev. J. I. Packer, M.A., D.Phil., Inter Varsity Fellowship, 1961, p. 112 f.

4. Ibid., p. 113.

5. *Readings in St. John's Gospel*, by William Temple, ibid., p. 269.

6. See my own 'Way' booklet for boys and girls called *Belonging*.

7. Fay Inchfawn, Freshford, near Bath.

8. *What to Teach and How to Reach the Young*, by George Goodman, p. 1, Pickering & Inglis.

Chapter Eight THE AGE OF ACCOUNTABILITY

1. *The Acts of the Apostles*, by G. Campbell Morgan, D.D., Pickering & Inglis, 1924, p. 219 f.